By the Author

How I Turned $1,000 into $5 Million in Real Estate—In My Spare Time
(Originally *into $1 Million*)

How to Make a Fortune Today—*Starting from Scratch*

My Odyssey Around Three Worlds

Nickerson's No-Risk Way to Real Estate Fortunes

William Nickerson

Simon and Schuster *New York*

*This publication is designed to provide accurate and authoritative
information, not legal advice. Events and laws may change after publication.
The author and publisher specifically disclaim any liability, loss, or risk,
personal or otherwise, which is incurred as a consequence, directly or
indirectly, of the use and application of any of the contents of the work.
Before acting on any suggestion presented in this book, legal or other
professional assistance may be advisable.*

Copyright © 1986 by William Nickerson
All rights reserved
including the right of reproduction
in whole or in part in any form
Published by Simon and Schuster
A Division of Simon & Schuster, Inc.
Simon & Schuster Building
Rockefeller Center
1230 Avenue of the Americas
New York, New York 10020

SIMON AND SCHUSTER and colophon are registered trademarks of
Simon & Schuster, Inc.
Designed by Irving Perkins Associates
Manufactured in the United States of America
10 9 8 7 6 5 4 3 2 1

Library of Congress Cataloging in Publication Data
Nickerson, William.
    Nickerson's no risk way to real estate fortunes.

    Includes index.
    1. Real estate investment.   I. Title.   II. Title: No risk way to real estate
fortune.
HD1382.5.N53   1986   332.63′24   86-15457
ISBN 0-671-55143-4

TO MY
GRANDCHILDREN
Bryan, Eric, Krista, Peter, and Tamara

Contents

6. NEGOTIATING FOR A SECOND FIXER-UPPER PROPERTY   60

7. JAZZING UP INTERIORS   72

10. OVER A HALF MILLION IN TWENTY-ONE MONTHS

13. THE SILVERADO TRAIL TO $1 MILLION IN 3 YEARS   155

14. CAREFREE SEMIRETIREMENT WITH HONEST PROPERTY MANAGERS   175

15. EFFECTIVE MANAGEMENT IN TODAY'S MARKET   189

16.   THE WRIGHTS FIND A POT OF GOLD   213

17.   OPPORTUNITY IS ALWAYS KNOCKING   239

Introduction

THERE ARE MANY obvious ways to make a fortune.

One is to gamble. You might get rich overnight.

But gambling is not a sure thing—that's why they call it gambling.

There are other speculative, get-rich-quick schemes—like buying real estate with dangerous nothing-down balloon-payment financing and bleeding, rather than improving, the property—but most easy-money fantasies turn into nightmares, and breed negative losses instead of positive profits.

By far the surest road to a fortune that can match or surpass your golden dreams is to buy, with sound financing, fixer-upper properties that you can improve.

You can choose from millions of deteriorated or obsolescent properties with repair and improvement challenges that you can readily correct.

Many owners just do not have the gumption to fix up wounded properties that have bled their lives away with age and neglect. If you have a little courage and imagination, you can buy such distress properties at a bargain, correct imperfections, and make a sure and spectacular profit. This gives you a built-in safety factor that guards you against going wrong.

If you faithfully follow my principles it is just about impossible to go broke. The only question is not whether you will make a profit, but how much you will make!

Basically, you can do modestly well by riding inflation. However, you are not going to make consistently good profits merely by floating lazily along with inflation's tide.

Inflation will increase property values an average of about 5 percent a year for the foreseeable future, but that is chicken feed compared with minimum profits of at least 100 percent for every dollar you invest improving property. In fact, the possibilities are very good, as I will show you by specific examples, that you can make 500 to 1,000 percent profits that can speed you on your way to becoming a millionaire.

"Just how can I actually become a millionaire?" you may wonder. "What are the secrets of success?"

The following chapters will show you step by step, starting where most real estate fortunes begin, with fixing up a single-family home. Then you will learn many money-making secrets, including the negotiation of bargain purchases, improvements, and financing, to help you earn fabulous profits that can make you a realty millionaire in just a few years.

This book will cite examples of actual accomplishments that you can surely emulate if you sincerely apply yourself. (The names of my students are changed to protect their privacy.)

I look forward to your following the surefooted money-making fixer-upper guidance in my books, and joining me and thousands of my students in the gratifying ranks of happy real estate millionaires and multimillionaires.

WILLIAM NICKERSON
MONTEREY BAY

CHAPTER 1

What Is
The American Dream?

MY WIFE, LUCILLE, and I were in Moscow not long ago and our friendly Russian guides talked excitedly about an exhibit put on by the American government at which a robot gave automatic answers to certain questions.

One of the most frequently asked was "What is the American Dream?"

"All persons shall be free to seek a better life for themselves and for their children" was our official government answer, but the robot did not give away one of the true foundations of the American Dream—a better life through homeownership and income-property ownership.

"Jesus said, "Seek and you shall find."

We can all be thankful that this free-enterprise land of America offers not only the freedom to seek a better life, but also abundant opportunities to find it.

MANY THOUSANDS HAVE FOUND SUCCESS

Many thousands of property owners have written to tell me how well they are doing in real estate investment after reading my books, especially my all-time best-seller *How I Turned $1,000 into $5 Million in Real Estate—in My Spare Time*.

Thousands have also told me personally at seminars, lectures, and TV and radio appearances how they started with almost nothing and made their first million in five to ten years.

BUY ONLY FIXER-UPPERS

From my millions of readers not a single person has ever stated that he followed my advice and it didn't work out. It's true that some have gone off on tangents deviating from my proven formula and not done so well. Several disappointed neophytes have told me of going broke, buying property with zero money down and short-term balloon payments, and doing nothing to increase value but wait for inflation. But I know of no failures who have followed the loss-proof safeguard of my number-one guideline: *Buy only property that you can improve, with sound financing*.

ALL IN A DAY'S MAIL

Everywhere I turn, I come upon examples of my money-making principles at work. In one recent pile of mail I received three letters from investors who all said they were doing well, and thanking me for showing them the sure way to become wealthy in real estate.

The first letter was from a college student of nineteen in Boston. He read only a few chapters of *$5 Million* in the school library and couldn't wait to finish my book. He went shopping and bought a money-making run-down duplex house at a bargain price of $49,000. His only down payment was an agreement to fix up the property.

The second letter was from an Atlanta couple in their early thirties who started investing with no money in the bank, but with good credit and vigorous ambitions, and made a quarter million in two years.

And the third letter was from a retired Eugene, Oregon, couple in their sixties. They started with a few hundred dollars five years ago and their net worth was already over a million.

SHUN NEGATIVE ADVICE

Time magazine states that half of my books warn you what not to do, so I'll give you an example of negative advice you should not pay any attention to. This was in a fourth piece of mail, an ominous form letter from a perennial Gloomy Gus forecaster. A year previously he predicted that there would be a complete economic collapse and our present financial world as we know it would come to a devastating end in six months! By then the government would start printing new money and would completely repudiate all outstanding money, government bonds, and other debts.

This last letter gave the same old pessimistic garbage that the U.S. economy was going to hell, and all stocks and real estate would be worthless. Gloomy Gus's advice was to stampede from the sinking American economic ship, sell everything you own at a sacrifice, and put all your resources into gold and diamonds and Caribbean bank accounts. About the only difference in the letters in a year was a switch from recommending Swiss bank accounts to the more fashionable Caribbean banks.

Of course, most of these doomsday forecasts never happen. As Calvin Coolidge said, "If you see ten troubles coming down the road, nine of them will run into the ditch before they even reach you."

WHO TO BELIEVE?

Have you received these discouraging Gloomy Gus letters? Who are we to believe? Should we believe this crybaby who says there are no more opportunities? Like Chicken Little he keeps hollering that the sky is falling. And sad to say, he has already gone bankrupt following his own advice! Or should we believe the world is full of opportunities, and that the best advice to follow is from the multitude of real estate investors who have actually made their fortunes?

I like to look at corroborating figures and found them in my copy of *U.S. News & World Report*, which also came in that day's mail. It might help you to decide whom to believe. The magazine's 1986 survey stated that by the end of the year the number of net-worth millionaires in the United States would reach one million, one for every hundred households. Let me repeat— one million solid-gold millionaires. In 1986 alone, while Gloomy Gus says there are no more opportunities, there would be over 100,000 new millionaires created, most of them in real estate. Just think, that one-year figure is close to twelve times the total number of 8,500 millionaires when I started! And another survey reports that there are over five million investors who are now considered wealthy because they are worth over $300,000.

ALWAYS SOME SOURPUSSES

Every day in history there are always some sourpusses who say the days of opportunity are over. But there is usually some sweetness in every sour note. For one thing, these pessimists leave more bargains for realistic investors who follow my guidance. You can happily take advantage of the mushrooming opportunities that are always there in real estate—sometimes better in good times, but always available in good times or bad.

I say let the gloom-mongers drown their hypochrondriac sorrows in their own debilitating tears. They are bound to worry about themselves, but don't let them bother you. Don't let them discourage you when you hitch your wagon to a real estate star and set a worthwhile goal to become rich.

Real estate opportunities today for the average person are greater than they have ever been. In different areas opportunities may vary, but there is some degree of real estate opportunity in every community. This includes your hometown area, where the grass is usually just as green and opportunities just as tremendous as anywhere else.

Real estate opportunities are assuredly there waiting for you and can dramatically change your life from a discouraging just-getting-by or lackadaisical coasting-along to independent wealth and ecstatic happiness with your accomplishments. America is a land where anyone who really wants to can become a millionaire, or a multimillionaire as I have, so you can enjoy just about anything you really want to. This includes writing your own book about your investment experiences, as have a number of my friends and colleagues, including Bob Allen, Mark Haroldsen, Al Lowry, and Howard Ruff.

OF COURSE, YOU MARRIED MONEY

Teddy Roosevelt said, "Real estate is the surest and safest road to financial independence."

Andrew Carnegie estimated that 90 percent of millionaire fortunes are made in real estate.

Most millionaires don't publicize it unless they happen to write books about their success. My friends had no idea of the extent of my holdings until my first book, *How I Turned $1,000 into a Million in Real Estate—in My Spare Time*, came out. Then many said, "Of course, you got your start by marrying money." The funny thing is, that's what others tell my wife! To set the record straight, Lucille and I were both stone-broke when we married. We were working our way through Fresno State College in Central California and decided we might as well marry and work our way together.

$15 A WEEK INTO $1,000 NEST EGG

My wife and I craved security because we both came from poor families. We asked our economics professor for suggestions on savings and investment, and he said, "Forget it! There's no use trying to save. The days of opportunity are over, and nobody can make a fortune anymore. The most you can look forward to is Social Security and, if you're lucky, a small company or union pension."

We paid no attention to this advice—except that we decided not to take any more economics courses! We were determined to save a nest egg for future investment. At that time we had no idea where to invest. I was selling Realsilk Hosiery door-to-door in the depths of the Depression, and we couldn't save a dime on my uncertain commissions. So I applied at several companies and finally got a steady job in 1933 with the Pacific Bell Telephone Company in Oakland, California.

I said, "I'll take any job but selling. I'm sick and tired of pushing doorbells selling Realsilk." So, naturally, they hired me as a salesman, selling telephones to people who didn't have any. In order to spread the work the phone company hired me at the lowest wage allowed by the government. That was $15 a week. Then when I started training they said, "While you're learning, it will be only $12 a week."

That reduced starting income turned out to be a lucky break. My wife and I figured out a budget to live on the $12. When we got the big raise to $15, we put the extra $3 every week into savings. I earned more raises and bonuses as time went on, and in three years we saved $1,000. I can assure you, saving a nest egg is by far the hardest task on the road to a fortune. The chief incentive for saving is the goal ahead, like dangling a carrot in front of a balky mule to encourage it to go forward. It's much easier when you progress from saving to investing and you own tangibles you can actually see, like houses and apartments, to spur you on.

PAINTED APARTMENT, THEN BOUGHT HOUSE

While we were saving our $1,000, Lucille and I fixed up the small apartment we were renting in East Oakland. The lower half of the walls were black with varnish. We removed this to expose the light oak underneath, then painted the rest of the apartment with cheerful colors. We also put in new curtains and drapes and a modern light fixture.

Our landlady, an elderly widow, was skeptical about our work as young amateurs. But when we finished she said, "Why, this looks beautiful. I'll paint my other apartments the same way." Then she said, "This makes them worth more." And she was right.

She raised all the rents—including ours. She increased the annual income by $960 and paid only $280 to a neighborhood handyman for labor and paint.

I calculated that she made a 343 percent annual return on her investment. That's what pushed Lucille and me into buying our first property. We were babes in the real estate woods and didn't know at the time that the resale value was increased by $9,600, over 3,000 percent of the cost. But a big profit was obvious. We told ourselves, "If you can increase values so much with this little money and effort, why don't we buy a place of our own and fix it up?"

Lucille shopped during the week for houses that needed fixing up, and I checked her selections on weekends. We bought a run-down house that was basically sound, using our savings for the down payment and for renovation costs. We painted inside and out and put in new plumbing and electrical fixtures and complete landscaping. This all increased its value, of course. In two years we traded our house equity for a basically sound duplex that needed painting and other cosmetic work.

We had found that fixing up our little apartment dramatically increased its value, and our landlady did us a favor by raising our rent! It was a case of casting your bread upon the waters. For we stumbled into an almost foolproof formula for making money—by just following the three R's of Renovating, Remodeling, and Refinancing. We had no spectacular goals in mind, like making a million. In fact, we were shooting for a side income of $100 a month by the time I retired from the phone company with a modest pension at sixty-five. When we started investing we were seeking only a minimum financial security, but we found financial independence beyond our wildest dreams.

HALF A MILLION BY FORTY-TWO

On a hit-or-miss basis and doing most of the improvements and maintenance work ourselves in our spare time, we invested in more apartments. We had no guidance except our own intuition to follow. There were no helpful real estate books or seminars at that time. In fact, real estate editors call me the grandfather of real estate authors!

When I was forty-two I made up a financial statement in connection with more borrowing and found that our net estate had mushroomed to over half a million. I saw a Dun & Bradstreet report about the tribulations of corporation heads who made over $100,000 a year, including some phone company presidents. Their chief worry, with high income taxes eating their salaries away, was whether, when they retired at sixty-five, they would have a sufficient estate to take care of themselves and their families in comfort.

I decided there was no reason to treadmill anymore for the phone company. What started as an investment tail was now wagging the wage dog, as my net rental income was ten times bigger than my salary.

The phone company was a good outfit too work for. There were many good friends, and I appreciated having a job that gave me a chance to save and establish good credit. A steady income helps your credit a lot, especially when you start investing with small savings. But it was one of the sweetest moments of my life when I was able to say, "Dear Boss. I quit!"

FRIENDS WANT TO KNOW HOW WE DID IT

My wife suggested, sweetly, that I take advantage of my early retirement and keep my real estate investment activities as a spare-time operation. "Then you can spend most of your time writing books to help others, as you've always wanted to do," she said.

I had several books in mind, and a big file cabinet full of notes on the characters I'd met while working in the Bell System, but knew that my first book had to be a guide to help others onto my sure path toward real estate riches.

Friends and relatives asked how they could imitate our success, so they could retire early with an independent income. I started writing down their questions and my answers and soon built up quite an investment file. The same questions were often repeated, and that is how my first book got started—more or less in self-defense. I figured if others asked these questions, I could say, "Look it up in the book!"

GIVING SECRETS AWAY

Many have asked, "Why are you giving your secrets away?"

There are two major reasons. For one thing, I have always wanted to be a writer. In college I took only one economics course. I studied mainly how to be a writer and preacher so I could devote my life to helping others. I never dreamed of being a millionaire and writing and preaching the gospel of free enterprise to encourage others to do the same. It seems that writers like to tell everything they know. I am one who shares this inner urge, so my life is an open book.

For another thing, I believe there is plenty of room for all who are interested in real estate investment. Too much of the country's assets are being swallowed by big corporations and big government. All investors and the country as a whole will be better off if as many people as possible know how to reap the fruits of free enterprise and share in the American Dream.

Successful people used to keep their secrets to themselves. They were afraid if they told how they made money, then the other fellow would get ahead of them. Now most enlightened property owners and realtors believe as I do and are glad to share their hard-won knowledge through their books and seminars and property owners' meetings.

It is certainly healthier for the whole economy if widespread property ownership is encouraged. This has always been the case in the United States, and property owners in the last sixty years have doubled in percentage, from a one-third minority to a two-thirds majority.

REFORMED COMMUNIST

In real estate, as in other areas, there are the haves and the have-nots, and a telling example of how ownership affects outlook was relayed by Winston Churchill, who complained that his gardener used to be a dreamy-eyed Communist.

One day the gardener said, "I stopped going to those party meetings. I don't believe that crazy stuff anymore."

Churchill asked for an explanation and the gardener said, "At the last meeting they said they wanted to take the money away from everybody who owns a thousand pounds or more, to divide it among those who have less."

"Wasn't that always their idea?" asked Churchill.

"Yes," replied the gardener, "but now I have a thousand pounds!"

CHAPTER 2

Why Doesn't Everybody Make Money?

YOU DON'T NEED any lucky breaks to make money in real estate. You don't need a particularly high IQ. You don't even need a large nest egg to get yourself started on your real estate fortune. All you need, I constantly tell audiences when I lecture, is average intelligence and average luck to make a million in real estate. Your savings can even be below average and you'd still have every chance of making it big.

At this point the disbelieving audience will turn and ask, "Then why doesn't everybody make his fortune in real estate?"

SIX SPECIAL ATTRIBUTES

I figure that you do need to develop six special attributes for maximum success. They are ambition, imagination, courage, persistence, judgment, and willingness.

Let me emphasize that you don't have to be born with these attributes. All of them can be developed and made stronger. All you need is to accept meaningful education and motivation like that my books strive to give you.

AMBITION

First, you need the *ambition* to get ahead financially. Some people just don't give a damn! Some perfectly healthy young people have told me that they are satisfied to stay on welfare and let the taxpayers support them all their lives. It is certainly worthwhile to set your goal to become wealthy, so you can do the things you want to do. And so you can contribute more to the welfare and economy of the United States and the world.

IMAGINATION

Second, you need the *imagination* to see the tremendous opportunities awaiting you if you follow my guidance in real estate investment today. There are many who, like my college economics professor, never in their lifetimes see an opportunity until after they have passed it by.

COURAGE

Third, you need the *courage* to make up your mind, to overcome your fears, get off the fence and do something. Obviously, you can't go anywhere until you get started. Have you noticed that some procrastinators always find an excuse to do nothing?

Anyone who faithfully reads my books already possesses some degree of these first three attributes of ambition, imagination, and courage. You have proved this by committing yourself to spend the time to add to your investment education. Then what else is needed for maximum success?

PERSISTENCE

Fourth, you need the *persistence* to keep duplicating my plan. Some get off to a fine start, then slacken. Some may find early satisfaction. Some may need a little more encouragement. How far you want to go is chiefly a matter of your personal choice. If you want to make a million or so, you have to keep making progress, like Norman and Karen Wright in later chapters. As Calvin Coolidge said, "Nothing in the world can take the place of persistence."

JUDGMENT

Fifth, you need *judgment*. Some get so enthused about how easy it is to make money in real estate that they think they can do as well in any field. Then they may disregard my tried and true precepts and wander off on a wild, speculative, money-losing tangent, like a nothing-down negative-cash-flow deal that leads to bankruptcy. A rather extreme example was given me by a Chinese restaurant owner who phoned from San Francisco. He said that he got so hopped up after seeing my book ads in the *Chronicle* that he invested $1,000, as I did. But he lost it all in one night.

I asked, "How in the world did you do that?"

He said, "I invested it in the dollar slot machines in Las Vegas!"

For sure success you do need the judgment to continue following my proven real estate investment principles that give you such a big advantage.

WILLINGNESS

Finally, you need *willingness*. For maximum success you need to apply yourself to money-making improvements. The magic key to maximum real estate success is a willingness to fix up property, correcting physical deterioration and/or improving management.

DON'T KEEP YOUR NOSE TO THE GRINDSTONE

You don't have to do any physical work unless you prefer to. You can hire it all, including management, as detailed in Chapter 14. To go forward the furthest and the fastest you do need to be willing to supervise or spend some of your own time and effort to arrange and oversee improvements.

Keep following my leadership in buying and improving fixer-upper properties and you will certainly be able to join me and thousands of my students in the ranks of multimillionaire real estate investors.

This doesn't suggest that you should keep your nose to the grindstone! Most successful investors find they can concentrate better on making progress if they frequently take time out for leisure.

SPECULATION VS. INVESTMENT

Another often repeated question is "What is the basic difference between speculation and investment?"

Investment property pays an income to help carry itself right from the beginning while you are making improvements to increase its value.

Buying anything with no income is pure speculation. This applies to vacant land, to gold and silver, and to diamonds.

One way to make money is to "buy wholesale and sell retail." With diamonds it's often the other way around. A friend bought a diamond from a dealer at a so-called "big discount." Soon after, he needed to raise money, and the same dealer would only pay half what he had charged for the diamond.

Some make a killing on speculative property, perhaps buying

vacant land by the acre and holding until they sell it as subdivision lots. But many guess wrong on the direction of subdivision growth. Or they may wait too long. Interest, taxes, and assessments can eat up all profits, as they cost about 20 percent a year nationally on vacant land. Speculation might profit those with sufficient income to "feed an alligator," but is not sound for total use of funds.

Of course, if you build new, competitive income property on land, as many are successfully doing, that is another way of improving property that can be a good investment. So is improving run-down farmland. But your first investment should be a property that needs fixing up, but has a foundation of proven rents. After you gain experience operating property with proven income, then you might consider building competitive new structures.

ODDS FAVOR OWNERS

After telling me about losing $1,000 in the slot machines, the San Francisco restaurant owner said, "I want to follow your advice and buy apartments here in the Chinatown area. I'm going to get your book and read it. But I'm a gambler at heart and like to know the odds on any deal I get into. What are the odds against me on property investment?"

I said, "As pointed out in my books, the odds are not against you, but strongly for you. Both government and insurance company studies show that if you take out a mortgage to buy property, the odds are four hundred to one in your favor that it will be paid off."

This is twenty times surer, by the way, than taking out a life insurance policy; one in twenty policies is canceled for failure to keep up payments. By contrast, if you start a new business, according to the Department of Commerce, the odds are four to one that you will go broke. Thus your chances as a property investor are 1,600 to one better than if you start a new business. A typical new business prone to failure is opening a restaurant.

AVOID RISKY PROPERTIES

I'm often asked, "What is the riskiest real estate?"

In general, any overfinanced property, bought with little or nothing down, where the loan is too big for you to make the payments.

About the worst specific sucker bait for the average investor is buying a resort. It is commonly easy to lose everything. There is a telling anecdote that demonstrates why most resort owners fail to make money. A reporter asked two resort owners, "What would you do if I gave you $1 million?"

One resort operator said, "I'd quit work and go fishing every day, take it easy and live off the income the rest of my life."

The second owner said, "I'd just keep on running my resort till my million was all gone!"

Some bold investors make money in resorts, especially if they have a large family and all members work their shirttails off. But resorts in most localities suffer from two major diseases—*seasonitis* and *weekenditis*. They are empty off season. And because of fast highways, fast autos, and fast living, many are empty during the season, except on weekends. The average resort runs about 90 percent vacant nationally on a year-round basis. Hotels and motels average about 35 percent vacant, whereas apartments nationally run only about 5 percent vacant.

"NOTHING DOWN" TURNED INTO FORECLOSURE

The riskiest real estate in general involves overfinanced property, bought with little or nothing down, with loan payments that are too big for the owner to make, either in a balloon payment or on a monthly basis.

A typical risky example was cited by a student at one of my recent lectures. He said, "After I attended a local real estate seminar, I took the teacher's advice and bought a rental house with nothing down. I paid a little over the market because I got 100 percent financing. The loan payments exceeded the rent, and I had to pay expenses out of my pocket. I didn't have any savings—spent every dime I made. I was going to pay the extra house costs from my salary, but then I lost my job.

"The seminar teacher said that inflation would push the value up at least 10 percent a year. I didn't have to turn a finger to increase value but could just wait a few months for inflation to push up the rent, so I would have enough income to pay my expenses and my loan. Then I could go ahead and buy another house. The teacher said all I had to do was buy one house a year for ten years and inflation would automatically make me a millionaire.

"After I bought the house, inflation came down to less than 5 percent a year. Expecting to increase value without making improvements turned out to be wishful thinking. I couldn't raise the rent and I couldn't make my payments, so I got foreclosed. Now I've got a new job. I'm saving my money until I get a few thousand put away, and I plan to follow your idea of buying fixer-upper property so I can realistically expect to increase values and make a good profit."

Of course, big double-digit inflation may return, but it is folly to make investment decisions based exclusively on that assumption. This is just one of many roadblocks on your path to fortune building.

WHAT IS THE SUREST ROAD TO A FORTUNE?

Your chief worry should be to fight bureaucratic attempts against free enterprise. Many odds in the property owner's favor can be preserved as long as we band together to join and support effective realty groups like Apartment Associations at the local, state, and national levels to challenge government encroachment.

Your odds for success are bound to be enhanced if you belong to an Apartment Association and attend its meetings, conventions, and seminars. This source of knowledge and experience will help you learn far more than the average owner.

There are many ways, of course, to make a fortune, but investment in fixer-upper rental dwellings is the surest road, meeting a vital necessity of life. It is actually rather difficult, I can assure you, to miss making money in home and apartment investment as long as you follow the suggestions and examples presented to you in this book.

A BOAT NAMED OPPORTUNITY

Opportunity comes not necessarily to those who wait, but to those who know where to look for it and what they're looking for.

Consider the case of one anxious young man who ran frantically down the dock, jumped across a stretch of water, and sprawled on the deck of the boat in front of a crowd of passengers.

"I didn't want to miss the boat," he said to the confused onlookers.

"What's your hurry?" asked a sailor. "This boat's coming in."

CHAPTER 3

The Perennial Boom
in Real Estate

SINCE MY EARLIEST success in real estate I have been extremely careful not to lead my questioning friends and relatives astray, but to give them only proven information so it was almost impossible to go wrong. I answered every specific question. But several asked, "What is the underlying secret to know we're on the right track?"

I was unable to answer. There was such a forest of details I couldn't chart a clear path so that anyone, no matter how inexperienced, could find the way. I asked others who were successful, and all they could give me was advice like "Keep your nose clean" and "Keep your nose to the grindstone." The only thing specific to follow was your nose!

The prevailing wisdom at the time was typified by a remark by billionaire Henry Kaiser at a symposium of business leaders on "What's the Secret of Success?" Kaiser stated, "The one who works the hardest at his present job is bound to rise to the top."

Kaiser's answer was sincere, I'm sure, and willingness to work is important. But if that is the secret of success, then the hardest-working laborer should always become the company president! I could not figure a better answer, and pondered over this underlying mystery for several months. I kept thinking about it while studying various references in my office in the mornings and working afternoons in my acre garden in the San Ramon Valley.

$1 MILLION FORMULA

Then at three o'clock one morning I awoke with a clear-cut, step-by-step formula in mind, spelled out as simple as the ABCs. Many inspirations that answer puzzling questions have come to me in the middle of the night. Another example is my two-for-one improvement formula—every $1 you decide to spend on improvements must increase value at least $2. Usually the increase in value by judicious improvements is much more.

I have learned that it pays to study a problem, then put it aside and let your subconscious help find the answer. When an answer comes in the middle of the night, it pays to get up and write the inspiration down. You can sleep better afterward, and your solution is still there and not lost in the cold light of morning. I'm no mathematical wizard, but something told me this formula would work out to $1 million. I got up and checked it on the calculator in my office in my home, and sure enough, it topped $1 million.

Most of you are somewhat familiar with my formula, as many other writers have copied it or referred to it. But much has changed since I first put pen to paper, so I will review my formula, slightly updated. For example, as it came to me it took an average of twenty years to make $1 million. But now it is more common to make it in five to ten years. Although prices have gone up considerably, that is only relative, and the formula still works and will always be a true guide. This we know from the many thousands who have followed it and already become millionaires.

You could start today with $1,000 as my wife and I did and buy income property. Many have told me recently that they have bought a rental house or duplex with little or nothing down. One of our apartment managers bought a brand-new duplex with nothing down and with no handicaps like balloon payments. He arranged to do the painting in place of a down payment.

There are many advantageous ways to arrange 100 percent financing as long as you can safely repay your loans. Another of our experienced apartment manager couples bought over $2 million worth of property with nothing down but their notes! It was, of course, fixer-upper property. They made advantageous improvements which immediately established a positive cash flow, and in just a few years sold for over $1 million profit.

AVERAGE SAVINGS AND AVERAGE LUCK

But for a sound start in today's market, I figure the average investor should have a minimum nest egg of about $5,000. That is the average savings on a nationwide basis for a typical family whose breadwinner is between twenty-five and thirty-four. Most older investors, especially professional people, have bigger nest eggs.

In this typical example, $5,000 would be the result of two years' savings at $200 a month, including some interest. You don't have to possess $5,000 cash in the bank if you have reserve equities or good credit. Most homeowners can readily borrow $5,000 or more on their home equities, and most employees with steady jobs can borrow from their banks or credit unions. And it is getting more and more common for relatives to lend the down payment to help buy property, especially a home.

I want to emphasize that my $1 million formula is not based on unusual expectations, but on average savings or credit and average luck for anyone who follows my guidance. Here is the way it works out:

BUY A FIXER-UPPER

You take your $5,000 nest egg and pay 10 percent down to buy a run-down but basically sound fixer-upper rental house. You thus borrow nine times your down payment, making a total of $50,000. There are myriad ways to arrange the $45,000 loan. Most simple is to borrow it all from the seller or a lending institution as a first mortgage. About one-third of all housing sales are completely or partially seller-financed.

Where the first mortgage falls short of required financing, a common practice is for the seller to grant a secondary mortgage to make up the difference. When necessary to complete financing, realtors may grant a third mortgage, covering their commission. And so on, into many hundreds of combinations.

IN YOUR SPARE TIME

While getting started with a small nest egg, this would usually be a spare-time investment, like mine while I worked for the phone company. You fix up the property, with your own or hired labor or a combination, painting and renovating and modernizing fixtures. You pay operating expenses and loan payments from the rents and plow back into improvements the net income, plus, in this example, your $200 a month in savings. It is important to continue saving in the initial stages, it helps a great deal to speed your progress, especially if you start with small savings. I've seen a number of fast starters slow down after buying their first rental property because they expect to immediately live like millionaires!

After the property is fixed up, it is worth more to a tenant, so you raise the rents, sometimes in an overall boost and sometimes in several steps. For example, you might install a wall heater or room air conditioner and raise the rent $100 a month. You increase the overall income an average of 25 percent. This increases the sales value 25 percent, as income-property values are traditionally based mainly on income. The national safe yardstick for apartments is ten times the net annual income.

ALWAYS DEMAND TWO FOR ONE

Remember my two-for-one formula. On your home what you spend is a matter of personal preference, but on rental or resale property you can't afford to be carried away by personal preferences. Every $1,000 you spend on improvements should increase value at least $2,000, every $1 at least $2. Otherwise don't do it! This gives you an ample safety margin in case you miscalculate. I know of many improvements that have increased value fivefold or even tenfold.

In twelve months you sell or trade for the increased value at a gross capital profit of 25 percent. As shown by later examples, this proves to be a nominal return for your imagination and effort. You pay sales costs, which average about 5 percent. I advocate buying and selling through realtors and paying their regular fees. They usually start at 6 percent on smaller properties and scale down on larger properties. Realtors will help you go faster and farther than you can go on your own. At the end of twelve months, after paying sales costs, you would have a net worth of $16,775. Then you turn around and trade this equity for a larger income property, perhaps four to eight apartments, again with average financing of nine times your down payment.

MAXIMUM FINANCING—THE VERY HEART

Many friends said they feared going into debt, and most new investors are afraid to borrow. In school Shakespeare taught us, "Neither a borrower nor a lender be." It is sound not to borrow heavily for personal pleasure, for then you are only a money consumer. But it is sound to borrow for investment to make money. Maximum financing is the very heart of making money, because you thereby earn a profit on the savings of others. This is the way that banks and other lending institutions make money, normally charging a reasonable fee in exchange for their essential services. When they take your savings they are money wholesalers, and you become a money retailer when you borrow from them for investment. Then your tenants who pay you rent are the ultimate consumers.

Some nothing-down buyers go broke by borrowing more than they can safely pay back. But many make the mistake of borrowing too little when they invest. For faster progress you want to harness maximum leverage and borrow the most that you can safely handle on each new long-term mortgage. The only safeguard you need is that you can repay loan payments plus expenses from your income.

I often reiterate that it's absolutely impossible to make a fortune today without the power of OPM. An oriental realtor in Hawaii asked if I was talking about opium. As most of you know, it's "other people's money"!

YOU MIGHT TURN OVER FASTER

I am often asked, "Must I follow your formula exactly in order to succeed?"

Of course not! It is a guide to show you the potential anyone can emulate. I know of many profitable resales within a few months of purchase. And you might make a bigger profit, as I know of many recent deals with profits between 50 and 100 percent. Such investment profits have been made throughout history.

Remember the Parable of the Talents way back in Bible times when a 1,000 percent profit was cited by Jesus? A master gave his three servants talents—we call them nest eggs today—to invest while the master was gone on a journey. One employee buried his talent, and nothing happened except that it got moldy. Two of the servants invested their money. The master returned to find that one made a profit of 500 percent and the other 1,000 percent. Thus Jesus emphasized that your money will lose value if you just bury it, and resources should be put to work by investment.

I previously mentioned how our landlady increased value 3,000 percent of her improvement expenses by only painting. Paint usually pays off more than any other improvement. Another example was proudly described by a white-haired fellow who got up after my lecture and said he read my book when he had only $400 in the bank. He was over sixty-five, drawing Social Security, and he couldn't wait to save more. He bought a dilapidated house for nothing down except a written promise to paint. Then he painted inside and out, and in one month sold his self-earned equity for a $4,000 profit. This made a 1,000 percent profit in just one month, or 12,000 percent a year!

A FAIRLY CONSERVATIVE FORMULA

We'll get back to my relatively conservative formula of an average 25 percent per year gross capital profit in an average turnover time of every twelve months. In twelve more months you would be worth $50,629. In one additional year, three years after your start with $5,000, you would be worth a net of $147,959.

Note that in this average example your progress with a small start is gratifying, but usually slower than later. That is why many investors get discouraged. Even though they start off fairly well, they don't keep at it. My proven formula is not a get-rich-quick scheme, but a get-rich-stick-to-it process on a sound plan for maximum success. After all, it does take some time to build a solid pyramid, just as it took twenty years to build the Great Pyramid of Cheops.

You can start your pyramid at any stage you are able to. With $150,000 for investment, you would be at our three-year level. One investor told me of putting $30,000 down into property after reading my book and turning it into a net worth of $250,000 in fourteen months. After two or three years of plugging along and laying a sound base of experience, you find it's much easier to handle larger properties, and you do start moving faster.

At the end of four years you would be worth $427,783, and at the end of five years you top a million with $1,232,277. If you keep applying yourself, at the end of six years you have a net worth of $3,545,197, and in seven years overall you top $10 million with $10,194,842!

Does this seem a little fantastic? I invite you to calculate it yourself, and you will see that it actually works out. In fact, many of my students have actually made their first $1 million in five years, and a number have become multimillionaires within ten years. In the next and later chapters I will show you details of just how Normal and Karen Wright made their millions and how you can do the same.

GOALS MAY DIFFER

You've heard the expression "Different strokes for different folks." Well, every investor has his own objectives when considering an investment. For every person who sets his sights on a $500,000 return, there's another who'd settle for $1 million, and another who'd be unhappy with anything less than $10 million.

At a recent bookstore autographing, I eavesdropped on the conversation of two little old ladies, both keen on making their real estate fortunes.

"I already have $10,000, and I'd be perfectly satisfied if I only made $100,000," one said.

"I already own a duplex," said the other, "and I'd be real happy if I could just learn how to collect the rents!"

CHAPTER 4

How the Wrights Negotiate a 1,000 Percent Fixer-Upper Profit

MENTIONED PREVIOUSLY WERE examples where owners made 3,000 percent and 1,000 percent profits by merely painting.

A 1,000 percent profit is also the net profit a middle-aged Metropole couple, Norman and Karen Wright, made on a run-down single-family house, mostly by transforming the exterior.

A CHALLENGE TO BEAT NICKERSON

Christmas of 1980, Karen gave Norman a copy of the just-published third edition of my *How I Turned $1,000 into $5 Million in Real Estate—in My Spare Time*. On the blank page at the front of my book Karen wrote, "Wouldn't it be fun to try to beat William Nickerson's $1 million formula?"

The Wrights had gained a little experience improving their own home, and decided to follow my recommendation to buy run-down property and fix it up. They had previously toyed with the idea, but kept putting off taking any action until they read my book. They made a New Year's resolution to start looking in earnest for potential good buys in January.

By depositing $200 monthly through payroll deduction they

had $5,600 in their credit union account that they were willing to commit if needed for a down payment or to help pay for improvements.

A DILAPIDATED-LOOKING HOUSE

The Wrights found a dilapidated-looking six-room house that seemed to be the worst on the block in a moderately desirable neighborhood on Spruce Street. The house obviously needed painting inside and out, and the yard was overgrown with untrimmed shrubbery.

An almost hidden sign in the front yard invited:

FOR SALE
TRY HARDER REALTORS
To Buy Or Sell
Phone 893-7111

At the Try Harder office a vivacious saleswoman, Patti Arthur, stated that the Spruce Street property was listed for sale for $33,500.

"It's worth twice that with a little fixing up," Patti Arthur said. "The owner, Mr. Stanley, is asking $12,500 down, which will cash him out to the balance of about $21,000 on the first mortgage. It's a good loan that's been there for a while. The monthly payment is $200 including only 8 percent interest.

"Mr. Stanley got transferred out of town and is anxious to sell. He tried to rent for $500 a month, but nobody wanted to live in a house that needed painting so bad. So he has no rent income to help pay his taxes and loan payments."

Karen Wright told the saleswoman, "The seller should spend the money to fix up the property or take the cost off the sale price."

Norman Wright said, "We'll have to have our contractor look the place over before we decide to tackle all the repair and improvement work that's needed."

A handyman contractor, Jack Armstrong, had satisfactorily

completed several improvement jobs on the Wrights' home, like adding closets and replacing a sink and a central furnace. The Wrights asked him for an estimate to paint the Spruce Street house inside and out, prune the shrubbery, clean up the yard, and make necessary minor repairs. Armstrong gave the Wrights a firm bid of $4,500.

EVERY ITEM IS NEGOTIABLE

After reading all the examples in my book, the Wrights realized that every item in a sales agreement is subject to negotiation, and it usually pays to make somewhat drastic initial offers in order to leave more maneuvering room.

Norman told Mrs. Arthur, "We're willing to take that run-down property off the owner's hands by just assuming the first mortgage that you said was $21,000. That means we would have to start making the $200 monthly payments, and the seller wouldn't have to worry about them anymore."

Karen said, "We need to save our money to pay for all the fixer-upper work, so we can't pay anything down."

The Wrights' objective was to get both the lowest price and the lowest cash down, so their funds on hand could be used to pay for improvements and help buy additional property. After some back-and-forth dickering they finally negotiated a purchase agreement with the following terms, and were able to take possession of the Spruce Street property on March 10, 1981.

NEGOTIATION SAVES $7,500 IN PURCHASE COST

Persevering negotiation reduced the sale price to $26,000.

As part of their purchase contract the Wrights agreed to assume the existing first mortgage with a balance of approximately $21,000. The Wrights also included in the written agreement their offer to pay for necessary painting and yard cleanup work, to be completed in ninety days.

Try Harder Realtors' 6 percent commission, payable by the seller, came to $1,560, which Mrs. Arthur said they wanted in cash. They agreed to take $560 in cash, which represented the Wrights' entire cash down payment. The balance of $1,000 plus 10 percent interest was to be paid by the Wrights in one year or when the property was resold, whichever came first. The Wrights signed a note accordingly, secured by a third mortgage, representing a credit of $1,000 to the seller and a loan of $1,000 from the broker to the buyer to help pay for improvements.

The seller had demanded all cash for the down payment, then partial cash. The Wrights induced him after further back-and-forth negotiation to postpone any payment so they could use the $3,440 the seller was due to pay for improvements.

The Wrights covered the $3,440 by signing another note for that amount, secured by a second mortgage, payable to the seller, including 10 percent interest, all payable in one year or when the property was sold, whichever came first.

The Wrights were able to obtain these favorable terms, giving them a total of $4,440 to pay for improvements, by emphasizing that the property was losing money and desperately needed work, and that they wanted to use their funds to pay for this work rather than further encumbering the property. They said that they expected to complete the fix-up work and sell within six months, at which time they would pay off the second and third loans. The loans would be paid in full in twelve months if the resale was not completed by then.

TWO CRUCIAL MONEY-MAKING DECISIONS

The Wrights made their first crucial money-making decision when they decided to buy fixer-upper property. They made a second crucial decision that would also affect how fast they made a million or whether they made a million at all.

They could take the slow-freight route of doing most of the improvement work themselves, by paying for labor and material only as sufficient funds were generated from rental income.

They chose to take the fast express to a million by financing and contracting all projected improvements as quickly as possible.

Jack Armstrong completed his improvement contract in two months. The Wrights decided to try trading the transformed house for larger property, and if they couldn't make a satisfactory trade, to sell.

In order to take advantage of existing capital gains tax treatment in case of sale, the Wrights decided to rent the house until six months from the date of purchase had elapsed.

On May 16, 1981, they leased the property at $850 monthly for one year to the Fisks, a couple with two daughters, aged thirteen and fifteen. The Fisks did not object to the proviso included by the Wrights in the lease agreement that a new owner could cancel the lease if the property sold.

THE TENANTS WANT TO BUY

The hottest prospect to buy a single-family home is often a tenant. Tenants may be eligible for most favorable financing, like 5 percent down, not only in houses, but also in duplexes, triplexes, and fourplexes.

When the Spruce Street tenants paid their rent on June 15, Mrs. Fisk said, "Our girls like the new high school they're going to. They've made a lot of new friends and hope they don't have to move again until after they finish high school. You said when we rented that you planned to sell the house. How much do you think you would take for it?"

Mr. Fisk added, "If you give us a good price we might buy it."

Norman Wright answered, "After all the money we spent to fix the place up we expect to get $99,000."

Mrs. Fisk said, "Well, that sure seems high."

Mr. Fisk asked, "Being as you wouldn't have to pay a commission, couldn't you see your way clear to give us a better price?"

"We would usually have to pay a commission, all right," said

Karen. "On a $99,000 sale that would come to about $5,000."
"We could give you credit for all the commission," said Norman. "That would bring your price down to $94,000."
"That still seems too high," said Mrs. Fisk.

NEGOTIATING A FAVORABLE SALES AGREEMENT

The Fisks and the Wrights arranged to meet the following evening at the Spruce Street house and attempt to reach an agreeable compromise. At a third meeting an agreement was finally made to sell at $89,000, with the following terms.

The closing date on which the Fisks would become legal owners would be September 15, 1981, so the Wrights could take advantage of capital gains tax treatment. Until that date the Fisks would continue to pay the $850 monthly rent.

The Fisks would pay 10 percent down, $8,900 in cash, and obtain a new loan for the remainder. The sale was contingent on their securing a loan of $80,100.

The Fisks' income enabled them to obtain an FHA loan of $75,000. They told the Wrights that they could not make up the loan shortage of $5,100 by paying more cash. The Wrights agreed to adjust the down payment by rounding out the cash down to $9,000 and taking back a second mortgage of $5,000, payable at $100 monthly, including 12 percent interest.

THE WRIGHTS GENERATE $58,738 IN CASH PLUS A $5,000 NOTE

The Fisks' rent paid for minor repairs, the $200 monthly payments on the old first loan, and the Wrights' share of escrow charges.

The Wrights received the net proceeds of the new $75,000 loan after paying off all three existing loans. The old first mortgage had been paid down to $20,600. The $3,440 second mortgage to Mr. Standey and the $1,000 third mortgage to Try Harder Realtors, plus 10 percent interest of $222 for six months, totaled

$4,662. This made total payoff deductions of $25,262, leaving the Wrights with a net of $49,738 in cash from the $75,000 loan.

Adding the $9,000 down payment totaled $58,738 in cash. The $5,000 second mortgage and note taken back by the Wrights generated $63,738 net assets as a result of investing a $560 down payment for their original purchase plus $4,500 for improvements, making total costs of $5,060. The Wrights' net profit came to $58,678, or 1,160 percent of their costs.

SURPASSING MY FIVE-YEAR $1 MILLION FORMULA

My formula in Chapter 3 showed you how to make $1 million in five years. The goal was to start with $5,000 and turn it into $16,775 in one year and into $50,629 in two years. These totals included the investors' putting in $200 a month of their own money for twenty-four months.

After closing the sale of their Spruce Street property, Norman and Karen Wright summarized their investment position.

"In six months," said Norman, "we have built our $5,060 investment into a net worth of almost $64,000. We're way ahead of Nickerson's $1 million formula."

Karen said, "Nickerson advised to keep saving, so we kept saving $200 a month in our credit union by payroll deduction. We haven't touched it after putting up the $560 down payment and the $4,500 for improvements. That left us with $540, so now our credit union savings have built to over $1,700."

"We had some extra good luck," said Norman. "We had a good, cheap worker like Jack Armstrong to handle our improvements. And we found a tenant who wanted to buy, so we saved sales costs."

"We made a good start on fixer-upper property," said Karen. "All we have to do is follow the same pattern till we make our million."

"I doubt if we do anywhere near as well on our next moves," said Norman. "But we'll sure keep trying."

CHAPTER 5

How to Make Fast and Sure Profits with Judicious Improvements

MANY SO-CALLED income properties pay no income, like the empty Spruce Street house when the Wrights bought it. They actually suffer more outgo than income, discouragingly losing rather than earning money, and thus decreasing in value.

Other properties keep making more money with the passage of time and, like the improved Spruce Street property, may spectacularly increase in value.

Why such a marked difference?

The answer is fairly obvious. Building values are lost for lack of improvements, and sure and fast profits are made with judicious improvements.

Two major money-making improvement factors are improving management, and physical improvements, including rehabilitation, conversion, and modernization.

I continually explore and apply these factors, and each division could readily fill a book. We will outline them all in this book. Later chapters will survey profitable interiors, government-sponsored rehabilitation, and basic management. This chapter will concentrate on the importance of other physical upgrading with money-making general and exterior improvements.

BLEEDING PROPERTY LOSES MONEY IN THE LONG RUN

Although we will always have periodic ups and downs in the economy, you can expect continuing inflation to increase the value of your property an average of about 5 percent a year for the foreseeable future. But there is a big *if*—this will happen *if* you keep your property improved, including modernization.

Remember the colossal national need for improvement. About fifty million dwelling units are over twenty years old and could stand some updating and improvement, and twenty million of these housing units need major rehabilitation. This inevitable obsolescence creates money-making opportunities if you buy run-down property like the Spruce Street house and fix it up or modernize property you already own.

Every day relentless time wears away at existing buildings. And we all know of some careless tenants who do more than their share to speed up the normal process of aging! Housing is a living entity. If you bleed it or neglect it, housing will decay and can eventually cost you money to bury it, as it may join the half million neglected units that fall below the slum line each year and have to be completely rebuilt or demolished.

GETTING PHYSICAL

Physical improvements naturally divide into two main categories, exterior and interior. I will not deal with them so much in theory as in proven experience by many thousands of students and by myself over a fifty-year period. For I am often asked by people seeking further guidance, "Just what do you do yourself to modernize your properties?"

I am not interested in expanding further to buy more properties, as I like to spend as much time as possible encouraging others through writing and lectures. But I join the realistic mortals who find it impossible to achieve perfection. Regardless of forethought and experience in planning, as soon as a new or renewal job is completed I always see ways in which the work could have been bettered.

As the years keep deteriorating all property through wear and tear and obsolescence, the potential for overcoming age by making desirable improvements is a never-ending process, and I keep at it. My estate has been aided by capital gains profits, tax-free reinvesting of net income, and continuing inflation. But sustained improvements have been the major factor for increasing the net value of my holdings to over $8 million from the lone $1 million when the first edition of my book, then titled *How I Turned $1,000 into $1 Million in Real Estate—in My Spare Time*, was published.

So I will mention chiefly some specific examples of improvements that I have actually tried and found profitable or have personally observed.

INVITING EXTERIORS

Your best silent salesman to help you sell or rent is the property itself. While desirable buildings and grounds invite prospective buyers and tenants, an uncared-for exterior repels them, leaving a property vacant and producing no income, like Spruce Street when the Wrights first saw it.

The big first in exterior needs is painting. Keep it up. Don't let paint fade and wear away until it shows heavy peeling and cracking. And point up any brickwork to keep it watertight and attractive.

Try to turn repair jobs into improvements. Whether working on exterior or interior repairs for single-family homes or multi-unit apartment buildings, keep looking for more ways to make profitable improvements.

Don't just patch or replace a roof to make it leakproof. Try also to improve the appearance. You can dramatize by using shingles, shakes, tile, slate, or composition shingles that look like slate.

Do exterior walls look beat-up, with cracks and splotches? Instead of only patching and painting, consider resurfacing. You might cover all or partial walls, exterior and interior and in atriums, corridors, and patios, with accent trim or siding, such as applications of stucco, brick, tile, aluminum, stainless steel, natural or simulated granite or marble, white, colored, or smoky glass, or plastic Plexiglas, shakes, shingles, or panels.

PANELING POSSIBILITIES

Types of panels are endless, with some examples in metal, glass, stone, and wood. Wooden panels may display natural colors and grains of many woods, including ash, birch, cedar, knotty pine, mahogany, maple, oak, redwood, and walnut.

Consider adding brick, tile, or colored concrete decks or trim to porches, balconies, landings, or walkways. For shelter from the elements and improved appearance, cover exposed entrances, or modernize them with bright canvas, glass, or plastic canopies, or aluminum or wood roofs, depending on climate and design.

Breathtaking accents can sometimes be exposed by scraping away decades of plaster layers from old buildings and uncovering unique mural artistry.

Attractive rustic window frames can be preserved, or windows can be modernized by aluminum or other replacements of many types, including casement, pivoted, projected, and double-hung models.

PLEASING LANDSCAPING, POOLS, AND WALKS

Landscaping can pay off tremendously, often increasing value by ten times or more what it costs. I spent $120 landscaping a duplex property, and in six months this transformation was appraised by a bank lender at $2,000, sixteen times its cost.

On one apartment project I spent $550 for landscaping, and the improvement was appraised by my bank two years later at

$20,000. The increase in value was, of course, aided by Mother Nature and a little tender loving care. For accent I planted tall shrubs and appropriate trees and used generous groundcover plants, not only for enhancement but also for easy upkeep and to help choke out weeds.

Landscaping adds a great deal of accent at reasonable cost where feasible at entrances, against exterior walls and fences, in atriums and patios, and on suitable roofs. In some areas artificial planting may be beneficial; for example, green outdoor carpets can be used for balconies and rooftop recreational areas.

You might be tempted to buy mostly large shrubs and trees, but bigness means escalating costs. Most of your plantings will get off to a good start and grow well with a little care if you buy them in gallon cans for a dollar or so apiece.

Your garden-supply house or neighborhood nursery can make good recommendations as to attractive plants that will grow well in your area with minimum care. With a little advice from the nursery you or your gardener or handyman can handle most planting and care. If you have a major landscaping project you might want a landscape architect to design and supervise its installation.

MORE GOODIES THAT ATTRACT HIGHER RENTS

With sufficient rental units to reduce the cost to a reasonable amount per unit—say twenty apartments or more—consider installing a swimming pool and/or wading pool. Or increase usage and enjoyment by adding a thermostat-controlled heater, preferably solar-powered, if there is none on an existing pool. In some energy-scarce areas, it should be mentioned, a pool heater is not permitted unless it is solar-powered.

Either with or without pool, consider individual or shared sundeck areas. Consider mini-streams, splashing waterfalls, fountains, and fishponds. I have added gurgling fountains in my downtown La Peralta Apartments and in garden-type suburban apartments at nominal costs, thus converting drab space into an inviting attraction.

Barbecues are a big hit with tenants, and so are hot tubs and saunas. Consider playground equipment if you cater to families with children.

AMPLE LIGHTING AND SECURITY

Inadequate lighting is a gloomy deficiency in most older apartments and in many new ones. Spot and flood lighting can brighten buildings and grounds and highlight entrances and walks, shrubbery, and recreation areas.

Pay particular attention to the entrance. Is it attractive and well lighted? Overall lighting also provides one of your best safeguards against burglary and vandalism.

How about the front door? It should be attractive and also provide substantial security. Directories and mailboxes should be well lighted and good-looking. Many owners are adding new strong locks to outside main entrance doors and giving each tenant a key.

Security measures are a growing national concern that has spawned a mushrooming use of security guards, patrols, and equipment. The number of private security guards exceeded a million in 1985, double the number of public police officers.

I have not only studied commercial security problems and solutions, but have served for twelve years as security chairman of our Homeowners Association, supervising professional patrols and safeguards.

I have provided better security in single-family homes, duplexes, and fourplexes by installing deadbolt locks on all exterior doors, securely locked windows, and ample lighting at the front door. I have installed speaker systems between shared front doors and each apartment in multi-unit buildings, so tenants can identify callers.

Most tenants are glad to pay extra rents for improved security.

At reasonable cost I provided reliable security at my hundred-unit La Peralta Apartments by installing:

1. a speaker system between the main entrance and each apartment, so each tenant can verify the acceptability of anyone seeking entrance;
2. a lock-release mechanism enabling each tenant to admit guests by momentarily releasing the main entrance lock;
3. a television monitoring system with a screen in the resident manager's office, wired to a camera overlooking the front door, so that whenever anyone rings the manager's buzzer she can look at the screen and speak to the party at the front entrance before releasing the lock; and
4. arrangements for tenants to connect their TVs to the monitoring entrance camera at a nominal charge.

THREE SURPRISED ROBBERS

Landlords often install elaborate security systems without any firsthand understanding of what it's like to be a victim in a break-in. That was indeed my situation, until shortly after I installed the TV monitoring system at La Peralta.

I was in the resident manager's office, looking at the new television screen, when the manager and I saw three husky men approach the main entrance.

One of the men buzzed the office. "I saw your ad in the paper for a two-bedroom apartment," he said over the intercom. "Me and my two friends want to see it."

"Okay," the manager said. "Come in." She pushed a button that released a lock on the front door.

The three men quickly entered the manager's office, demanded all of our money, and promised not to hurt us if we followed their orders.

"We don't have any cash," the manager insisted. "It's all in checks and won't do you any good."

"We'll decide that," said the one who had spoken on the intercom, who seemed to be the group's leader. "Give me your purse and hand over all the cash and checks you've got."

Then the leader turned to me. "Give me your wallet and empty your pockets," he instructed. "And be quick about it."

At this point I calmly called their attention to the new security system we'd just installed. "Every move you make is recorded on TV," I said. "Look at that screen."

The three men looked at the TV screen. We could see their surprise when they recognized, through the camera, the front entrance where they'd just been.

"Let's get outta here," the leader said to his cohorts. "Keep your face turned away from that TV."

Without saying another word, the three men turned quickly toward the main door, putting their hands over their faces as they passed under the camera's surveillance, and disappeared down the sidewalk.

The incident proves, if nothing else, that the very existence of a security system is sometimes enough to scare away would-be intruders. Though the police were unable to find any trace of the three men, our surveillance system succeeded in protecting us, and the facility, from any injury or damage.

CHAPTER 6

Negotiating for a Second Fixer-Upper Property

THE WRIGHTS CONTINUED having payroll deduction deposit $200 monthly in their credit union account, which pays 6 percent annual interest. For convenient availability and higher interest they deposited the balance of their funds in a money market account, which paid 10 percent annual interest.

The Wrights' Spruce Street profits and their savings gave them $65,478 for further investment. Their funds on hand enabled them to buy almost any size rental property they chose, from a duplex to a hundred apartments or more.

For faster advancement I advocate buying the biggest money-making property with the most financing you can safely handle. Safety means that your income property funds plus other available funds or credit can pay operating expenses plus loan payments while you are fixing up a property to sell or trade for a profit.

THE WRIGHTS DECIDE TO CONCENTRATE ON FOUR-PLEXES

Since their first investment experience on Spruce Street had turned out considerably better than they expected, the Wrights decided to coast somewhat below their potential. Like many beginning investors, the Wrights didn't want to strain their good fortune by pushing too fast. They felt they needed more experience with smaller apartment buildings, like fourplexes, before they ventured into larger ones with ten or more apartments.

The Wrights were open-minded about picking up a good fixer-upper buy between a duplex and six to eight units, but decided to concentrate on fourplexes. They answered for-sale ads in the *Metropole News* and looked over various properties offered by realtors.

The following ad immediately caught the Wrights' attention.

FIXER-UPPER
4-PLEX!
Double
your money!
Cindy Seekum
Go Far Realtors
Phone 464-3930

A loquacious Cindy Seekum showed the Wrights a faded pink stucco fourplex on Wildwood Avenue in a moderately good neighborhood. There was a tilted "For Sale by Owner" sign in the front yard.

Mrs. Seekum said, "The owners are a retired couple. They have been trying to sell this property themselves for almost a year. No results, as you might expect. So they have just signed a six-month exclusive listing with Go Far."

"How much could it be bought for?" asked Norman Wright.

"The sellers, the Duncans, started out asking $150,000. They were very hard-nosed about negotiating either the price or the terms. They demanded all cash of $70,000 to the $80,000 loan. They dropped their price to $140,000 before they signed up with Go Far. I talked them into listing for $130,000, and they have to pay a 5 percent commission out of that. They expected inflation to push up values more without keeping up the property. So they have let it run down. That makes it a good buy for fixer-upper investors like you."

A POSSIBLE GOOD BUY

"It could be a good buy if we get the right price," said Norman. "We'll have to check just how much work it needs."

The two-story Wildwood fourplex was composed of four identical two-bedroom flats, two lower and two upper. Each had a separate entrance in front and also a back door. Each flat had 1,200 square feet of floor space. The rooms were fairly large and included a 12-by-14-foot dining room. The tenants paid all utilities except water. The flats were all unfurnished and each rented for $275 monthly.

Mrs. Seekum gave the Wrights the following statement.

10727 Wildwood Avenue
Owner just slashed price to $130,000!
This is your chance to double your money!
SEE CINDY SEEKUM, GO FAR REALTORS

Loan balance approx. $80,000, payable $750 monthly including 8% interest.
Cash down $50,000 or refinance.
Gross income: 4 flats × $275 each;
    total $1,100 monthly   Annual $13,200

Annual Fixed Expenses

Taxes	$1,280	
Insurance	214	
Water	76	
Total	$1,570	1,570
	Net annual income	$11,630

Several yardsticks are usually employed in appraising property, covering income, replacement value, and sales of comparable property in the area. On the basis of ten times the net annual income the market valuation was approximately $116,000. On the yardstick of 100 times the monthly gross rent of $1,100 the market value was $110,000.

To replace the 4,800-square-foot building the going economical construction rate, in the area of $42 per square foot, would be $201,600. This would represent the replacement value if the property was fixed up in first-class condition. Depreciating 30 percent would leave a 70 percent depreciated valuation of $141,120. The lot would sell for about $35,000, making the total replacement value of the depreciated building and lot $176,120.

IS THERE A CHANCE FOR THE WRIGHTS TO DOUBLE THEIR MONEY?

Karen Wright asked Mrs. Seekum, "How did you dream up that 'double your money' idea? Isn't that a little wild?"

"Not at all. You've got a good sound building to start with, but it just hasn't been kept up. You could spend $20,000 or $30,000 and sell for close to double what you pay to buy the property. Similar buildings in good shape in this neighborhood are selling for nearly twice the Wildwood price."

"That might be double your initial cost," challenged Karen, "but not double your money including improvement costs!"

"We might consider it just the same," said Norman. "There sure is a lot of work that needs to be done. You'd have to completely paint the inside and outside. And all that scuffed and gouged pine flooring needs replacing."

"The place does have possibilities," said Karen. "I just hope it doesn't cost too much to fix it up."

"We'll look into it with our contractor," said Norman. "Then we'll see if we can make you an offer."

"Better not delay too long," warned Mrs. Seekum. "A person looking for a fixer-upper is bound to snap this up. Why don't you go ahead and make an offer? If I can get the seller to sign, it will tie up the property. You could put in the sales agreement 'Subject to buyer's approval of repair costs.'"

"If we did that we'd have to include 'buyer's approval of repair *and improvement* costs,'" said Norman. "Anyway, we'll have to study the whole deal before we decide to make an offer."

Norman believed there was some advantage to tying up the property. But there might be more of a cost disadvantage, as the seller would expect a higher price than the buyer could negotiate by delaying the first offer.

The Wrights made a thorough inspection of the Wildwood fourplex with their previous contractor, Jack Armstrong, and reviewed desirable improvements with him. Armstrong said that he and his employees would do some of the work and some would be subcontracted. He obtained bids from various subcontractors, then submitted the following written estimate.

Improvement of Wildwood 4-Plex
10727 Wildwood Avenue
Metropole, Columbia

Change 4 2-bedroom to 4 3-bedroom flats
Transform 4 12' × 14' dining rooms
into 3rd bedrooms by installing ward-
robe closets across ends of rooms.
(Note: Ample space in kitchens to pro-
vide dining area.) $3,500

Completely paint interior and exterior
Includes preparation, patching, labor
and material.   3,700

**Cover all pine floors in living rooms &
bedrooms with wall-to-wall carpets**
Includes nylon carpets and rubber pad-
ing under all carpets.   3,950

New linoleum floor tile in 4 bathrooms and
4 kitchens   2,600

Modernize kitchens
Replace kitchen cabinets. Install new
stainless-steel sinks with disposals and
Formica counters.   3,400

Miscellaneous by contractor, repairs and
additions

Includes plumbing, replace 8 faucets,
2 per flat; electrical, add 8 outlets, 2
per flat; carpentry, replace bathroom
cabinets and repair windows, all 4 flats.   900

Landscaping, including yard cleanup   350
    Total all sub-bids $18,400
    Add 10% contractor overhead   1,840
    Add 10% contractor profit $1,840
    Total cost of above $22,080

Payment: Weekly progress payments as work is completed.

Armstrong said that he had obtained the best possible bargains
from all subcontractors. "You're welcome to check with other
contractors," he said, "but I'm sure they can't touch my price."

KAREN TRIES A LITTLE NEGOTIATING ON THE CONTRACT

Norman said, "Your price looks okay for the work that needs to
be done if we buy the property. Now that we have your bid, we'll
have to figure the potential profit and if the project is really
worthwhile."

"While we're figuring, it would be simpler to deal in round
numbers," said Karen. "Couldn't you make the total an even
$20,000?"

"That's impossible! I'd be losing money for my time," Armstrong said.

"I would think that you could at least knock off that $80 and
make it a round $22,000."

"I'll do you a favor and cut my profit. I'll make it exactly
$22,000."

FIGURING THE POTENTIAL PROFIT

The Wrights estimated that the transformed three-bedroom units could probably rent for $550, double their present $275 two-bedroom rental. However, they would play safe by figuring on the basis of a probably sure rental of $495, making $1,980 monthly. Using a valuation of 100 times the gross monthly rents would increase the market value to $198,000.

After discussing the possible results of adequate negotiation techniques, the Wrights estimated that they might be able to buy the Wildwood fourplex for $100,000, and they had a good chance of buying it for not over $105,000.

To the latter figure they added improvement costs of $22,000 and probable sales costs of $9,900 at 5 percent of the potential $198,000 resale price. All anticipated costs totaled $136,900. Deducting this from $198,000 would result in a profit of $61,100, or 44.6 percent. If they should buy for $100,000 instead of $105,000, the resulting potential profit would be $66,100, or 50 percent.

"It's a long way from our percentage profit on Spruce Street," said Norman. "But the amount is close to the same. And our expected profit on this deal is close to double Nickerson's 25 percent average profit goal if we buy for $105,000. We would actually double Nickerson's suggested goal if we buy for $100,000."

THE FUN OF NEGOTIATING

"That's all the more incentive to buy for $100,000," said Karen. "Let's give our negotiating a real try."

"You know, renting the new three-bedroom flats for $495 should be a cinch," said Norman. "And we have the possibility of renting for more. Of course, renting for more and buying for less would both make our profit even higher."

"Negotiating to do the best you can is fun," said Karen. "It's fun to see how low you can go without losing a good deal. Let's start with an offer of $80,000. And we won't pay a cent in cash, just offer to take over the loan."

"Negotiating is a game, like bluffing at poker," said Norman. "The other party never knows whether you're bluffing or not. But at each stage you've got to make them think you will not better your offer. We want to start as low as possible, but not so low that the other party gets mad and tells us to go to hell. Better start with maybe $85,000."

"Okay. Let's go for the $85,000 offer, but start with no cash. We'll put in our $5,000 Spruce Street note for the down payment."

The Wrights offered $85,000 for the Wildwood fourplex, with the provisos that they would take over the $80,000 mortgage and pay the $5,000 difference with their note, secured by a second mortgage on the Spruce Street house.

THE REALTOR PROTESTS LOUDLY

Mrs. Seekum protested loudly when the Wrights gave her their $85,000 offer: "Your offer is ridiculous! Your price is impossible even if you pay the $5,000 down in cash. The Duncans have always said they would never take back second mortgages. That is one reason, besides holding out for an unrealistic price, that they were never able to sell. It's a complete waste of my time to fool with this cheap offer of yours. Can't you raise your sights a little higher?"

The Wrights insisted on having their $85,000 offer submitted to the Duncans.

The next day Mrs. Seekum advised the Wrights, "The Duncans absolutely refused to consider your time-wasting offer. They said your price was insulting. But I talked them into making a counter-offer of $120,000, all cash down to the first mortgage. This means only $40,000 cash down, and your $5,000 note is out. I think they are giving you a bargain, and you'd better take it without any more delay."

MORE NEGOTIATION GETS GOOD RESULTS

The Wrights had been discussing their next offer. Norman told Mrs. Seekum, "We've been thinking about all the work the place needs, and we're getting discouraged about buying."

Karen said, "We have to keep the price down to make up for all the work that has to be done. But we'll raise our offer to $90,000. And we've decided that our $5,000 mortgage note has to be part of the down payment."

Norman said, "We've got to save our funds to pay for all the improvement work. The other $5,000 to make a total down payment of $10,000 would have to come from the Wildwood property. We'll give the Duncans a second mortgage of $5,000 on their fourplex."

Again Mrs. Seekum protested. "You're still way too low in your offer. And you know the Duncans have refused to take back any mortgage. As I told you, it's wasting my time and theirs to put that in your offer."

The Wrights insisted, as before, that Mrs. Seekum submit their new offer.

The following day Mrs. Seekum advised, "I didn't think the Duncans would reduce their price any lower. But I talked them into a new counteroffer of $115,000, all cash to the first mortgage. This means you only have to pay $35,000 cash down."

The Wrights offered $95,000, including for the first time cash of $5,000 to go along with the two previously submitted second mortgages of $5,000 each, one on the Spruce Street house and one on the Wildwood fourplex.

The Duncans reduced their price to $110,000, with a $30,000 all-cash down payment.

Norman Wright told Mrs. Seekum, "We have decided not to go over $95,000, with all the work that has to be done to fix the place up. But we will include $10,000 cash in our down payment to go with our $5,000 second mortgage on Spruce Street."

Karen said, "We are willing to forgo a second mortgage on

Wildwood. But we are determined to include our $5,000 second mortgage on Spruce Street, if we buy."

HONING A FINAL NEGOTIATION

Mrs. Seekum contacted the Wrights with the Duncans' response: "Mr. and Mrs. Duncan say they are sick and tired of your insulting offers. I talked them into reducing to $105,000, and they say that is final and rock-bottom. And the down payment of $25,000 must be all cash. You'd better accept this and stop fooling around or you'll lose your chance to get a bargain. What the Duncans are offering you now is a terrific buy."

Norman Wright said, "We have decided to go to $100,000 if everything else works out the way we want it. We're willing to increase our cash down payment to $15,000, but our $5,000 note on Spruce Street must be included in our total down of $20,000."

"This is the best we can do," said Karen. "You've got to include our $5,000 note."

"If the Duncans don't agree to this, we'll start looking for another buy," said Norman.

THE SELLERS TIRE

Mrs. Seekum returned from the Duncans with terms close to mutual agreement. "The Duncans are getting tired of bargaining. They want to close the deal and move to Arizona. They said you can have their property for $100,000, but your $20,000 down must be all cash, no ifs, ands, or buts. And they insist that you must accept this final offer within twenty-four hours or the deal is off."

"That's great that they have agreed to our final price," said Norman. "As we have told you over and over, our $5,000 mortgage has to be included as part of the down payment."

"You know they absolutely refuse to take back any mortgages," said Mrs. Seekum. "I don't know why you have to be so stubborn!

Why don't you go ahead and pay the $20,000 down in cash, so we can close the deal? Then you can sell your second mortgage to somebody else if you must get rid of it."

"That's a good idea," said Karen sweetly. "Norman and I have been talking about what we would do if you couldn't sell the Duncans on taking our $5,000 note. If we sell it to another party for cash we'd have to take a sizable discount, even though it's a good mortgage with plenty of equity. But a party to a sale like this usually gives full value."

ONLY ONE PARTY LEFT

"We insist that our $5,000 note be included in the deal," said Norman. "If you can't get the Duncans to take it, there's only one party left who would logically take the note."

"That's you," Karen said to Mrs. Seekum. "You'll lose out completely if you don't take the note. So we would appreciate your accepting it as your full commission. Then we can go ahead and close the deal."

Mrs. Seekum protested again. "It isn't right to stick me with your stinking note! Such an unlikely possibility has never crossed my mind. My boss and I both expect to be paid our commission in cash."

"You said the Duncans are giving you only twenty-four hours to close the deal," said Norman. "Instead of taking a chance of losing all your commission, why don't you get your broker's agreement, so we can all go ahead?"

"I don't think it will do any good, but I'll talk to my broker."

Mrs. Seekum and her broker agreed that it was better to accept the $5,000 note rather than wind up with nothing.

The Wrights turned over their $5,000 second mortgage on Spruce Street to the title company as their deposit. They then wrote a check for $15,000 to complete their down payment.

On November 12, 1981, the Wrights became the legal owners of the Wildwood fourplex. They told Jack Armstrong to start immediately on the contracted improvement work.

The $15,000 down payment from their money market account left the Wrights with a total savings balance of $46,869. Their money market account remaining balance was $44,709, including two months' interest at 10 percent. Their credit union account totaled $2,160, including two monthly deposits of $200 each, plus 6 percent interest for two months.

CHAPTER 7

Jazzing Up Interiors

THEY SAY YOU can't teach an old dog new tricks, but you can sure jazz up an old dog of an apartment house. We need only to look at the success enjoyed by the Wrights in modernizing the Spruce Street house and the Wildwood fourplex to recognize the handsome profits available to investors who are willing to modernize and improve their properties.

Interior modernizing possibilities are virtually unlimited, but in this chapter we'll explore some of the money-making specifics that I have tried or observed.

In the lobby and common halls consider painting, accent decorating, and lighting. Possibly you can use carriage or hanging swag lights. You can accent certain walls with wooden, marble, or imitation-marble paneling, and with paintings, murals, or tapestries. Consider sculptures and a live, babbling fountain.

Pay particular attention to lobby furnishings. Take out old, beat-up sofas and replace with a modernistic love seat or a wooden or marble bench. Attractive drapes or blinds in pastel colors and bright carpets can do wonders to transform a dull lobby. Ceramic tile or slate installed in eye-catching patterns is a real winner for lobby floors.

Long halls can be made more inviting when a tunnel view is segmented by latticed panels or other dividers, such as potted plants. The view can also be improved by wall lamps and alternating sections of flooring, with varying colors of carpet, for example.

INSIDE THE APARTMENT

Inside the individual apartment, I'll mention some overall suggestions, then some that apply to certain rooms. Soundproofing as an aid to privacy and quiet enjoyment is a major tenant desire. Party walls can be made more soundproof by adding Sheetrock, Celotex, or wooden panels on furring strips.

Consider adding dead-air space with a dropped ceiling where space permits, or add acoustical ceilings on furring strips. Wall-to-wall carpets installed over rubber padding cut down noise considerably. Brighter colors are the trend for carpets in living rooms, bedrooms, and interior halls.

Large mirrors, modern light fixtures, and heating, plumbing, and cooling appliances as additions or replacements should be considered throughout. Sometimes one single installation, like room air conditioning or a wall-mounted gas or electric heater, can modernize an apartment at reasonable cost and make it readily rentable at more profitable rates.

Consider adding thermostats if not already connected to heaters. Also consider dimmer switches in all rooms and concealed lighting indoors and out, replacing incandescent with fluorescent lighting inside and vapor mercury lamps outside. Security locks may be needed on windows and outer doors.

In the living room, interior halls and entry, and large bedrooms, consider adding mirrors and paneling a wall or two with Philippine mahogany or other inexpensive laminated wood. The attractive panels upgrade appearance considerably and are usually installed in 4-by-8-foot sheets, covering space fast and keeping total cost of labor and material low.

For a larger living room it pays to panel two adjacent walls for accent. For a smaller room one wall is usually sufficient. An attractive painting on one wall can add a great deal to appearance. So can drapes and venetian blinds or narrow-slatted miniblinds.

KITCHENS DEMAND CABINETS

Average potential renters usually go from the living room to the most remodeled room throughout the country, the kitchen, where they expect to spend many hours a day. Some studies show ample storage the most desirable interior design feature and inadequate storage the biggest tenant gripe. Try to install generous storage space with adequate cabinets in the kitchen and bathroom and adequate closets in bedrooms and halls. Remember that some bonus storage can be provided by hooks, towel bars, and narrow shelving on the backs of closet doors.

In kitchens, as at the Wildwood fourplex, install economic factory-made cabinets where needed to give more storage both overhead and under the counter. If there is an open space under the sink, cover it with cabinet doors to provide concealed storage and a more pleasing appearance. As at Wildwood, old, pitted countertops should be replaced or covered with ceramic tile or Formica. As at Wildwood, chipped or worn-out sinks should be replaced, and new swing mixing faucets should be installed.

Consider a breakfast bar in the kitchen or between kitchen and dining room or kitchen and living room. Colorful vinyl flooring tile, indoor-outdoor carpet, or linoleum as at Wildwood should also be considered. For added convenience, consider installing garbage disposers, and for added attraction, stainless-steel sinks, both installed in the four Wildwood flats. In higher-rent potentials, consider dishwashers. Also consider a ceiling vent fan. A copper-toned hood over the stove, with built-in vent fan and light, can do wonders to modernize the cooking area.

BATHROOMS DEMAND MORE CABINETS

The next stop is the bathroom. Install a modular acrylic shower stall or a modern tub with adjustable shower overhead if feasible and needed. On new and old tubs, install a shatterproof glass or Plexiglas enclosure to replace messy shower curtains. The wall above the tub, at least to shower level, should be covered with ceramic tile or marbelized Formica.

Take out old washbasins with exposed plumbing and install a ready-made cabinet with shelves underneath, concealed with cabinet doors, and with a Formica or ceramic-tile top. Replace old wooden or sheet-metal, usually vertical, medicine cabinets with wide, horizontal, single-shelf cabinets, the type with sliding glass doors and a fairly large mirror. Consider a full-length mirror on bathroom doors, facing either bathroom or bedroom, or possibly one on each side.

Bathroom floors give you a choice of hard or soft surfaces, as in the kitchen, depending on types of tenants and local preferences. You can install colorful vinyl tile or linoleum, as at Wildwood, or you can go the carpet route, either indoor-outdoor or tufted shag. The latter is popular in bathrooms, but impractical in kitchens.

WHAT ABOUT BEDROOMS, HALLS, AND DINING AREAS?

In bedrooms and entry and dining areas, consider paneling or attractive wallpaper on one or more walls. Also accent lighting, curtains, drapes, or miniblinds, and wall-to-wall carpets. Stay open-minded in looking for ways to increase storage. If closet space is small and the bedroom large enough, add a walk-in closet with sliding doors. An additional closet can often be built at the end of a hallway. Usually overlooked is usable storage space along the walls of wide hallways, where there is still adequate room for passage after you install bookshelves and cabinets 9 to 12 inches deep.

IS LAUNDRY EFFICIENT AND SUFFICIENT?

One-third of all tenants gripe about inadequate laundry facilities. Most apartment renters consider an efficient and adequate laundry a must. They want equipment that operates efficiently without frequent breakdowns. And they want sufficient facilities to meet normal tenant requirements without unreasonable waiting.

The Spruce Street house and the four Wildwood flats each had a small service porch that accommodated automatic washers and dryers. Such exclusive space is not common in individual apartments.

You should try to find enough space for a suitable laundry room for all tenants to use even if you have to give up a storeroom, workroom, or garage. Most older apartments are built with adequate community laundry space, and most older apartments also have dead space that can be readily converted. Architects traditionally plan sufficient space in new construction. Most laundry setups, old or new, can be jazzed up by keeping them clean, cheerfully painted, and well lighted, and by replacing older washers and dryers.

Newer washers operate efficiently without wasting hot water, and newer jumbo dryers handle bigger loads. Tenants love those big commercial machines that don't balk at bath rugs, beach towels, and terry-cloth robes.

Copy most prudent owners and make all laundry equipment coin-operated. Some owners expect to make a bigger profit by installing and maintaining their own machines. But they usually find that profits are devoured by high repair costs, pilfering losses, obsolescence, and out-of-service losses while waiting for the plumber.

LET A COMMERCIAL OPERATOR RUN YOUR COIN LAUNDRY

I prefer to make arrangements with a commercial company that specializes in installing and maintaining coin-operated laundries. Their radio-dispatched maintenance people are prompt when plumbing and equipment problems arise, and they can keep you supplied with up-to-date equipment that requires fewer repairs.

Many commercial companies will offer incentive bonuses to

landlords considering their services, and these bonuses usually come in the form of a fee to cover laundry-room enhancements such as painting, decorating, and the purchase of tables and chairs. I used most of the $1,500 bonus supplied by the company I hired to service the La Peralta Apartments to completely redecorate the laundry room there; I put in new marbleized walls that helped to give the room the look of a Roman bath.

Depending on the size of your facility, a commercial laundry company will pay you approximately 25 percent of the gross receipts on a fourplex community laundry, to a high of 50 percent on installations in larger facilities.

Be wary of companies that offer more than 50 percent on large installations; unfortunately, many commercial laundry companies lack the integrity you'll find in other businesses, and it's often a good idea to add extra safeguards to ensure an honest count. I've heard of laundry operators who report only half of their take to the owner, so a contract to pay 60 percent of the receipts results in only a 30 percent share. There are, fortunately, many honest companies from which to choose, and I've found an operator who uses tamperproof meters on all machines to record, automatically, the total actual receipts.

A good laundry arrangement not only pleases tenants, but can pay a fair net profit to offset the value of space and cost of utilities. The laundry operator at La Peralta mails me a monthly check averaging $300, about $3 per tenant.

Following is a copy of the Laundry Lease Agreement covering La Peralta Apartments.

OTHER COIN-OPERATED CONCESSIONS

Depending on location, number, and type of rentals, other coin-operated concessions may provide desirable service at a profit. Consider cold and hot drinks; candy, snack, and cigarette machines; play equipment, like pool and billiards and various other games; hair dryers, especially if you have a pool or hot tub; and public telephones.

LEASE

LA PERALTA LAUNDRY AGREEMENT

Date...January 7, 1981........................

This lease is between Web Service Co., Inc., hereafter called Lessee, and ...W. E. Nickerson..........,

Owner, or acting with full authority as owner's agent, hereafter called Lessor, of that certain property consisting of

..100... rental units located at 184 13th Street, Oakland, CA, known as La Peralta

..Apartments........................

1. Lessor hereby leases to Lessee the laundry room or rooms on the above premises described for a period of five (5) years from the date of this lease for the purpose of installing and operating its laundry equipment for use by tenants, all of which shall remain its exclusive property, be under its exclusive control, and shall be maintained by Lessee.

2. Lessee agrees to pay as total rental to Lessor a sliding scale commission based on the average per machine monthly gross income: WEB TO PAY 50% ON ALL INCOME, SEE ITEM #9 BELOW

    40% when gross income averages $27.00 per machine
    30% when gross income averages $22.00 per machine
    25% when gross income averages under $22.00 per machine

3. Number of machines shall be controled by Lessee. (Double-load machines to be counted as two.)

4. Lessee shall provide during this lease Bodily Injury and Property Damage Liability Insurance in the amount of $3,000,000.00 for each occurrence.

5. Lessor agrees to provide ingress and egress to the leased premises at all reasonable times. Lessor agrees to provide maintenance service for the leased premises and to provide all utilities necessary for proper operation of laundry machines without cost to the Lessee.

6. This agreement shall be binding upon and inure to the benefit of the heirs, executors, assigns, and personal representatives of the parties. Lessee may assign this lease. If any litigation results in connection with this lease, the successful party shall be entitled to reasonable attorney's fees.

7. This lease shall be subject to approval of the Home Office of Lessee, and shall become immediately effective upon approval, with or without notification.

8. The interest of the Lessee hereunder shall be subordinate to the lien of any future lender utilizing this property as security.

9. Web to pay a commission rate of 50%.

10. Web to pay a decorating allowance of $1,500.00 upon signature of
    agreement.

THIS LEASE SHALL BE AUTOMATICALLY RENEWED FOR THE SAME PERIOD OF TIME DESCRIBED IN PARAGRAPH 1 HEREOF UNLESS CANCELLED BY WRITING SENT BY REGISTERED OR CERTIFIED MAIL BY EITHER PARTY 60 DAYS PRIOR TO EXPIRATION.

PAY COMMISSION AND ALLOWANCE TO:

Name. W. E. Nickerson........................

Address 184 13th Street........................

..........Oakland, CA 94612........................

APPROVED BY: WEB SERVICE CO., INC.,
LESSEE: HOME OFFICE

By. Jerry Ludwick..........Date. 1-7-81.

LESSOR: W. E. NICKERSON, OWNER

By. X ....

OWNER

Title ....

When I worked for Pacific Bell I used to supervise the installation of public telephones, and I know that the phone company will pay you from 5 to 15 percent of the gross receipts, as at La Peralta, depending on the amount of usage. So don't let the phone company talk you into paying it for the service, as it is apt to, if your public telephone usage proves fairly heavy.

Tenants usually appreciate services like those listed, and the coin machines can also pay the owner a good additional profit. Owners may buy and install most of these facilities. The majority of owners, like me, find it advisable to arrange for professional operators to install all of them, along with laundries. In this event the owner receives a percentage of the gross receipts without any capital outlay or maintenance expense.

PROFITABLE ADDITIONS

Sometimes a comparatively modest addition can yield a gratifying profit, as with the previously mentioned room air conditioners and heaters. Perhaps one of the most lucrative additions, at low cost to the owner, is the installation of cable television. In some cities, like Oakland, cable television operators will pay the owner a bonus for permission to install free prewiring to all apartments. This helps them detect unauthorized hookups, but also encourages honest tenants by waiving their otherwise high installation charges.

In deluxe rental units, high rents can climb even higher with the installation of hot tubs, spa, bathtub with whirlpool jets, or fireplace.

I increased rent $500 a month in a desirable Sacramento duplex by installing a double fireplace in a custom unit at a cost of $2,250, paying for itself in four and a half months, and increasing capital value by $60,000. The multicolored used-brick fireplace had two faces, one into the living room with a hearth and mantel, and the other into the dining room with barbecue attachments. A fairly low 8-foot ceiling in the one-story garden-type apartment complex minimized the chimney-installation expense.

CONVERSIONS OF SPACE

Often costing one-tenth to one-quarter what new construction does is the reshaping or revamping of existing space. Most profitable is converting nonproductive or little-used space into additional bedrooms or other often-used space, such as a study or den. One of the most common ploys in residential areas is converting an enclosed garage into bedroom, family room, or den.

In single-family homes, duplexes, apartments, and all sizes of housing, opportunities are often there to considerably increase rents at small cost by converting a sizable dining room into a bedroom, as at Wildwood Avenue, and arranging a dining or breakfast nook in the kitchen, living room, or entry. Hallways can often be eliminated by removing a wall and blending the space into an adjacent room, converting the space into more profitable usage as a breakfast nook, for example, and/or closets and shelves.

Where some rooms are rented for transient sleeping, as at my La Peralta Apartments and the block-distant Hotel Oakland, the same space can be converted to more profitable apartments drawing long-term tenants. I have made this desirable change by installing compact kitchenettes, with a kitchen sink, stove, and refrigerator, and ample electric outlets to handle other appliances. City Hall okays this change if square footage is adequate. Where rooms are small I have created comfortable apartments by converting three adjoining rooms into two studio apartments, with the middle room partitioned in half. Each half-room is large enough to be equipped with a kitchen and connected to an adjoining room.

Several units at La Peralta suffered an awkward arrangement not too uncommon in older buildings—two sleeping rooms shared one bath between them. In most of these paired units, one room was usually vacant or experienced constant turnover. Why? The first tenant, usually a resident for several years, found it was possible to keep a private bath by making life miserable for the second tenant. Tenant number one tied up the bath for laundry, hair drying, and long tub soaks, and kept forgetting to unlock the other tenant's bathroom door on vacating. So tenant number two soon moved.

This uncomfortable, rent-losing situation was profitably remedied by creating a desirable one-bedroom apartment, converting one sleeping room into a living room with a compact, fully equipped kitchen.

FURNITURE AND APPLIANCES

My wife and I have found that putting in new furniture can modernize appearance and pay good profits in some higher-vacancy areas, especially during periods of overbuilding in a particular area. That's partially because most new units are unfurnished. Construction financing may include some equipment and amenities, but seldom covers most furniture costs.

The major ongoing trend nationwide is to rent unfurnished. A tenant who needs furniture expects to buy or rent it from a furniture supplier. Furniture-rental firms can provide fairly desirable items at reasonable charges because they routinely buy at factory discounts of at least 50 percent off the regular retail prices.

It's better to remove old furniture rather than save it. If it's salvageable, give it to your favorite charity that will pick it up, like the Salvation Army, Volunteers of America, or Society of St. Vincent de Paul. Otherwise turn it over to your junkman.

Adding furniture to smaller studio-type apartments often pays off better than any single item besides paint and landscaping. Usually the gross income can be increased enough to pay for the furniture in two or three years. I know of many cases where rents for one year or less have paid for all new furniture.

Regardless of your policy with standard furniture items, like sofas, beds, tables, and chairs, it is customary in most areas for the owner to provide required apartment appliances, such as stoves, heaters, and refrigerators. Tenants nearly always provide optional appliances, like freezers and microwave ovens. You should replace any stoves, heaters, or refrigerators that look ancient or beat-up, and renovate any usable appliances needing repairs.

MODERNIZING MAY SAVE OPERATING COSTS

Consider modifying utility arrangements, including energy costs for heating, lighting, appliances, and air conditioning. Modernizing may save significantly on energy costs. Tenants will conserve energy about 30 percent when they pay for it. Take a good look at the possibility of sub-metering utilities and transforming central heat and air conditioning to individual units. Both projects are detailed in later chapters.

Cost effectiveness should always be considered along with greater tenant convenience. Sometimes the costs of modernizing appear too great to warrant a change. This is often the case before you figure tax applications, which may convert an apparent money-losing project into a profitable money-maker. Tax considerations on specific projects will be covered in later chapters.

Insurance savings may offset costs of installing fire-discouraging sprinkler systems in halls and other common areas, like storage and laundry rooms. This is a possibility to keep in mind when considering the updating of plumbing.

JOIN YOUR APARTMENT ASSOCIATION AND BUY WHOLESALE

You can make bigger profits if you not only increase income but also reduce costs wherever feasible. A potential cost reducer often overlooked is buying wholesale instead of retail. Your local Apartment Association helps a great deal by sponsoring a monthly magazine with ads from suppliers who sell wholesale to apartment owners. At state and national Apartment Association conventions you have a direct pipeline to wholesale buying through scores of eye-opening exhibitions.

Visit every exhibitor that interests you and ask about the big discounts available to you as an Apartment Association member. I know of many cases where substantial discounts on furniture and appliance orders have been sufficient to pay all convention expenses, including travel. Happily, most of these expenses, like food, lodging, travel, and seminars, are tax-deductible for both husband and wife when they jointly own rental property.

On items like paint, furniture, appliances, and equipment, 25 percent to 40 percent discounts for apartment owners are common, with some wholesale prices running as low as 50 percent of retail. Even retail outlets like Sears and Wards and neighborhood hardware stores commonly give at least 10 percent discounts. But the discount is seldom volunteered. You have to ask for it. Usually the only credential you need as a wholesale buyer is your membership card in your local, state, or national Apartment Association.

Many prospective members join in the first place so they can buy at Apartment Association discounts. Just one purchase can often save considerably more than the nominal annual dues.

Besides providing education at conventions and seminars, one of the main purposes of Apartment Associations is to represent rental-property owners at City Hall, the county courthouse, and national and state capitals. Most Apartment Associations perform many other services, such as arranging substantial member savings for group insurance, fleet auto purchase discounts, and other programs.

IMPROVEMENT LOANS ARE EASY TO GET

About the easiest financing to obtain, even in a tight money market, is an improvement loan, available at most banks, credit unions, and savings and loan organizations. You can get improvement loans to take care of all your modernizing of buildings, grounds, equipment, and furnishings. Banks and other lenders will loan amounts far exceeding FHA maximums, and will usually give you as long as fifteen years to repay.

The increased income generated by improvements should pay off financing costs and add to your in-pocket income. Improvement loans used to cost about double the going rate for long-term loans, but now the premium is considerably less.

After you make the improvements and raise the rents, when the money market is favorable you may want to shop for a long-term loan to pay off all other loans. For example, pay off first and second mortgages, improvement loans, and chattel mortgages, if any, on furniture and equipment. This consolidation in one loan should considerably reduce your overall payments and increase cash flow.

With tight financing it is common to utilize a new wraparound loan to raise funds to pay off all short-term loans, which have proportionately high interest. The wraparound leaves intact the long-term, low-interest, and low-payment prior mortgage or mortgages.

Some savings and loan associations and banks will lend on the value of so-called personal property in addition to the building and land, which makes it easier to finance furniture and equipment purchases on a long-term basis.

There are many types of loans available using as security your equities in your home, your apartments, and other income properties. There are many sources to consider for short or long-term financing. It pays to shop for money as much as for other purchases, with credit unions, banks, insurance companies, building and loan and savings and loan associations, and mortgage brokers.

SAVE ON TAXES

Much of your refurbishing, such as adding furniture, carpets, and drapes and painting, does not require a permit. We all know that when you take out an improvement permit your property taxes are almost always increased, as the tax assessor adds the amount on your permit to the value of your property. This encourages the bleeder and discourages the improver.

There is much discussion and some implementation at federal, state, and local tax-making levels to have a five-year moratorium on taxing improvements, particularly in urban-renewal, redevelopment, or other close-in city areas.

From an income tax standpoint, you have always been able to write off your improvements much faster than regular depreciation. Much of your work, like painting both exterior and interior, can be written off the year of expenditure and charged to repairs on your income tax return.

Equipment and furniture, of course, can be written off fairly rapidly, between three and five years on the average. Even though your main building account is depreciated in eighteen or twenty years, a major apartment addition or remodeling can be written off in less time, say ten years, under present regulations.

One of the incentives in the new proposed laws is to allow you to write off all rehabilitation in five years, even major building remodeling. All rental-property owners should contact their appropriate federal, state, and local legislators to push for these taxing incentives that encourage property improvements.

HOW MUCH PROFIT SHOULD YOU MAKE?

I can't mention enough the importance of one of my many tried and true maxims—every $1 you spend for improvements should at least double your money and increase value a minimum of $2. When I'm asked by investors looking to spruce up properties how much profit they should make, I offer two answers. "Make as much profit as you can," I coach my students, "but don't settle for less than double your investment."

Obviously, there is no profit in spending $1 to increase value by only $1. If you estimate that the increased value will be at least double your outlay, then you have an ample safety margin in case you miscalculate, and you should still make some profit. In most cases, the judicious improvements I've mentioned in general, and the ones I've outlined specifically in the Wright's Spruce Street and Wildwood properties, will more than double your money.

CHAPTER 8

Uncle Sam Pays You for Rehabilitating Old Buildings

TAX CREDITS AND other deductions keep changing.

At this writing in 1986, Uncle Sam gives rehabilitation tax credits to encourage rehabbing nonresidential structures at least thirty years old, and for residential or nonresidential buildings that are Certified Historic Structures.

The residential rehabbing accomplished by the Wrights on Spruce Street and Wildwood Avenue would not qualify unless the buildings were Certified Historic Structures. Further details of rehab qualifications will be cited later in this chapter. For the present, as an example, I will outline the qualified rehab work that I undertook on my hundred-unit La Peralta Apartments in downtown Oakland, California. La Peralta was built in 1908, soon after the big earthquake of 1906 devastated the area.

There was a lot of dead space that paid no income. In fact, there were about 17,000 square feet going to waste in the capacious lobby and in the full basement that used to be stacked with tenants' trunks and crates. Because one of the laws of junk accumulation is that vacant space will always be filled, both the basement and screened-off lobby stored owners' and tenants' old sofas, mattresses, and other discards, waiting to be donated someday to the Salvation Army.

In a reasonably finished state suitable for commercial rental this dead space would compare favorably with property costing at least $60 per square foot to build, bringing the additional replacement value to approximately $1 million. However, the projected increase in immediate net annual income was in the range of $60,000, which would add about $600,000 to the capital value.

Applying my previously mentioned minimum formula requirement of a $2 increase in value for every $1 in cost, I determined that finishing the dead space in order to produce income would be a safely profitable project, without figuring tax savings, if the work could be done for a cost in the range of $300,000.

DOUBLE-CHECKING FOR ADDED BONUSES

Added bonuses would be gained by enhancing the entrance and the lobby by:

1. covering the atrium with new glass panels;
2. installing a bubbling fountain in the center of the core lobby;
3. installing a new ceramic-tile lobby floor; and
4. surrounding the lobby with accent shrubs planted in alcoves.

These enhancements would upgrade the general appearance, warranting a general upgrading of the rent schedule. A realistic estimate of this potential increase in income, particularly after including painting and refinishing the entire exterior, should be in the range of 10 percent. This would approximate $30,000 a year, further increasing the overall market value by about $300,000, or a total of about $900,000.

The more I checked the potential figures, the more evident it appeared that this prospective conversion of dead space into commercial rent-paying space was a sound $3-for-$1 project. My estimate of probable costs, based on previous experience, was about $250,000. If the work could be contracted in that range it looked quite profitable without considering the additional bonus of tax savings. My top federal and state income tax brackets would generate about $150,000 in tax savings, through depreciation and credits, making my net cost after taxes about $100,000. This would push my increase in capital value to nine times the net cost, or 900 percent.

MY ARCHITECT'S ESTIMATE AGREES WITH MINE

Since I planned to spend most of my time writing, lecturing, and traveling, I decided it would be worthwhile to hire an experienced architect. Working through an architect is an option open to any fixer-upper investor who prefers to hire improvement supervision. An architect versed in improving income property can design and supervise all improvement work advantageously, and can often save the owner more than the usual fee.

I asked an architect friend, Randy Borden, to give me his estimate, with the prospect of drawing the plans and supervising the project. He came up with a probable minimum cost of $225,000 and a possible maximum of $250,000, with the latter as an outside figure that should cover any unforeseen contingencies.

Borden said there should be no license or permit problems, as the city of Oakland joined with the state of California and federal housing agencies in encouraging the rehabbing of older structures.

This left only the question of financing. If the money could be obtained at reasonable cost, I would okay the drawing of the preliminary plans and a firm contract to go ahead. The going rate for a potential construction loan at the time was 14½ to 15 percent. I believed this to be higher than I might be able to obtain later. If loan rates didn't drop low enough to suit me, I could wait a few months until sufficient savings were built up from income.

STANDARD AGREEMENT WITH ARCHITECT

While considering the most feasible financial agreement, I told the architect to go ahead with preliminary plans. My standard agreement with the architect provided, in case no construction ensued, that he would be paid $40 an hour. For any other employees, such as draftsmen, I would be charged two and a half times their payroll cost.

If construction was financed and contracted, the architect would complete working drawings, obtain contractors' bids, and oversee the work. In this case the foregoing payments would be credited against a fee of 10 percent of total construction costs. The 10 percent overall fee would be disbursed as follows:

Upon completion of preliminary drawings	15%
Upon completion of working drawings and all necessary designs	20%
Upon completion of all construction documents, including detailed specifications	40%
Upon completion of contractor bidding and negotiation	5%
Upon completion of all construction	20%
Total	100%

A FORTUITOUS LETTER FROM BANK OF AMERICA OFFERS LOW-COST FINANCING

The architect had hardly started on the "preliminaries" when the mail brought a fortuitous letter from the Bank of America, which shifts between first and second in rank as the biggest in the world.

The colossal bank offered improvement financing at a comparatively reasonable cost of 12¼ percent, about 2½ percent below the going market. Attached was a detailed outline of

 **BANK**OF**AMERICA**

Community Development #3762
180 Montgomery Street, 19th Floor
San Francisco, CA 94104

October 26, 1981

W. E. Nickerson
La Peralta Apartments
184 13th Street
Oakland, California 94612

Dear Property Owner:

The City of Oakland and Bank of America are co-sponsoring
a special Loan Program, offering below market, fixed rate
financing for improvements, or for the acquisition and
improvement of residential rental income properties.
Attached is an outline describing the program.

Since funds available under this program are limited, we
encourage you to call the Oakland Main Office of Bank of
America or the City of Oakland for more information.

We look forward to hearing from you.

Sincerely,

Don Walsh
Vice President/Manager

Enclosure

BANK OF AMERICA — CITY OF OAKLAND
Multi-Family Residential Property Loan Program

Bank of America, acting as Lender under the City of Oakland Multi-Family Residential Property Loan Program, has available fixed rate financing for acquisition and rehabilitation or rehabilitation only of qualified multi-unit rental properties.

The purpose of this program is to restore, preserve, and maintain existing rental properties, in order to provide affordable housing units within the City of Oakland for low to moderate-income families.

INTEREST RATE AND TERMS

Purchase/Rehabilitation Loans:
  • Fixed Rate — 12.25%
  • Maturity — 15 years
  • Security — First Deed of Trust

Rehabilitation Loans:
  • Fixed Rate — 12.25%
  • Maturity — 15 years
  • Security — First or Second Deeds of Trust

Origination Fees — Loan Size $		% of Loan
Up to —	250,000	3.75
250,001 —	500,000	3.00
500,001 —	1,000,000	2.50
1,000,001 —	Up	2.00

Expenses and fees associated with the loan may be financed if the maximum loan possible provides sufficient debt service as approved by the Bank.

BORROWER/LOAN PROCEEDS

• Borrower may not occupy the project if it is a single-family dwelling.
• For projects which include both acquistion and rehabilitation, 20% of the total development cost must be expended on eligible rehabilitation work.
• Refinancing of existing debt is limited to 10% of the loan request.

UNDERWRITING CRITERIA

• Loan to Value Ratio—75% (After Rehab.)
• Debt Service Ratio—1.15 to 1 coverage

APPLICATION PROCEDURES

The Owner/Applicant should contact Bank of America for an appointment to review the project *prior* to submitting a loan application and financial package to the Bank for evaluation.

The Bank may be able to provide a two-phase application process as follows:

  • Based upon financial exhibits presented, the Bank would make a preliminary review and respond as to the probability of considering a loan application, subject to an updated credit review at formal application, favorable appraisal, completion of an Improvement Certificate (Parts I–V) and execution of Regulatory Agreement.

—and—

  • At formal Application, the Owner would submit an updated financial package as may be required and all construction documents to the Bank for appraisal and conditional loan approval. (Anticipated loan conditions would be compliance with all requirements of Bank's Appraisal Department, completion of all required loan documentation).

FOR ADDITIONAL INFORMATION REGARDING PROGRAM GUIDELINES OR LOCALITY REQUIREMENTS, PLEASE CONTACT:

City of Oakland
Lester Graves Lennon
Office of Community Development
(415) 273-3502

Oakland Housing Authority
Jeff Meyer
(415) 874-1546

FOR ADDITIONAL INFORMATION, LOAN INTERVIEW AND APPOINTMENT, PLEASE CONTACT:

Bank of America
Oakland Main Office
2000 Broadway
Oakland, CA 94612
Jack Clevenger
(415) 273-5221

the bank program, making a tempting offer that appeared unreasonable to refuse.

Following are copies of the Bank of America letter and accompanying outline from Community Development Vice President Don Walsh of the San Francisco headquarters.

CITY HALL AND THE BANK ENCOURAGE REHABS

I phoned the Oakland office of the Bank of America and was turned over to rehab specialist Greg Gillam, Assistant Vice President, Real Estate. I made an appointment and at his office outlined my La Peralta improvement project, with an estimated cost of $250,000.

Gillam said my proposal looked "entirely feasible." He said that Bank of America had contracted to supervise the rehabilitation program originated by the improvement-minded city of Oakland. Similar financial incentives were authorized by the federal government throughout the United States to encourage rehabilitation.

Nationwide housing and commercial construction projects were rehabbing run-down and vacant nonproductive properties to full use at a cost averaging about half that of new construction.

These rehab funds were raised from private capital at lower than market costs by making the earnings tax-free—untaxed both by the federal government and by the state in which the rehab money was used. General Accounting Office studies indicate that tax incentives originally cost about five cents for each dollar of rehabbing work generated. Besides conserving existing resources, the government eventually comes out ahead, as rehabbing greatly increases income on each improvement project. This results in higher income taxes to offset initial tax losses.

Investors in bonds which funded rehab projects like La Peralta received tax-free interest both federally and in the state of California. The so-called "municipal bonds" which provided funds to rehab owners like myself paid 10¼ percent to bond buyers. To an investor in maximum tax brackets like mine, 50 percent federal and 11 percent for California, this tax-free income was the equivalent of approximately 23 percent in taxable income.

USE REHAB FUNDS TO BUY FIXER-UPPERS AND PAY OFF ONEROUS DEBTS

To the municipal-bond payment of 10¼ percent, bank servicing costs averaging 2 percent are added, making the interest cost to rehabbers 12¼ percent. Previously, tax-free bond funds could be used only for rehab costs. But revised regulations permit using the mortgage funds both for rehabbing and for buying a building that needs rehabbing, with the proviso that at least 20 percent of total loan funds be expended for rehabbing.

The availability of so-called "purchase-money" funds opens the door to new fixer-upper buyers, like the Wrights in Chapters 4 and 6. New buyers can use the subsidized funds to pay the seller and also to pay off some existing loans. The latter action is especially desirable if there are short-term loans with relatively high payments. A maximum of 10 percent of the rehab loan funds can be applied to pay off existing debt, thus helping to consolidate financing, reduce monthly payments, and improve cash flow.

THE BANK LIKES TO BE FIRST

Gillam said that the bank preferred, of course, to have a first mortgage as security. But if there was sufficient property equity, as I had in La Peralta, the bank would consider a second mortgage, subordinate to the relatively low existing first mortgage.

Gillam gave me the bank's standard cost-breakdown form and asked that I have it filled out by my architect or contractor. My architect, Randy Borden, obtained bids and estimates from various contractors and subcontractors and filled out the bank form shown here, based on the minimum acceptable bid of $240,190. This included architect's fees of $21,800 for plans and supervi-

TO: **BANK OF AMERICA**   OAKLAND MAIN   251

Branch   No.

2000 Broadway   OAKLAND   Calif.   94612

LA PERALTA APTS. **COST BREAKDOWN**

JOB ADDRESS 184 13th St., Oakland, CA. 94612 FHA #

OWNER WM. & LUCILLE NICKERSON BUILDER

1. BUILDING PERMIT	1350
2. WATER METER	n.a.
3. SURVEY	n.a.
4. TEMPORARY FACILITIES	n.a.
5. DEMOLITION & SITE PREPARATION	2500
6. EARTHWORK	n.a.
7. CONCRETE FORMS	n.a.
8. STRUCTURAL CONCRETE INCL. FLRS.	n.a.
9. LUMBER—ROUGH	5600
10. LUMBER—FINISH	3500
11. CARPENTER LABOR—ROUGH	15400
12. CARPENTER LABOR—FINISH	8700
13. DOORS & FRAMES (incl. hdw.)	10250
14. WINDOW FRAMES & SASH (labor for each)	1000
15. CABINETS & MILLWORK	n.a.
16. HARDWARE—ROUGH L.S.	300
17. HARDWARE—FINISH (T. acces + misc)	500
18. PILING IN PLACE	n.a.
19. REINFORCING STEEL	n.a.
20. STRUCTURAL STEEL	n.a.
21. PLUMBING—ROUGH (incl. F. sprinklers)	8000
22. PLUMBING—FINISH	—
23. ELECTRICAL—ROUGH (incl. new serv.)	48000
24. ELECTRICAL—FINISH (incl. tenant fixt.)	
25. ROOF TRUSSES	n.a.
26. ROOF COVER	n.a.
27. STRUCTURAL MASONRY	n.a.
28. MASONRY VENEER	n.a.
29. STUCCO, EXTERIOR LS	800
30. SPECIAL EXT. WALL CONSTRUCTION	n.a.
31. HEATING, VENT., AIR COND. (incl #32)	15000
32. SHEETMETAL & FLASHING	—
33. GLASS & GLAZING	1500
34. LATH & PLASTER OR SHEETROCK	9320
35. INSULATION & SOUNDPROOFING	450
36. TILEWORK	9600
37. FINISH FLOORING carpet	7040
38. PAINTING & DECORATING	9400
39. SPRINKLER SYSTEM (see # 21)	—
40. ELEVATORS	n.a.
41. SHOWER DOOR	n.a.
42. BUILT-IN EQUIPMENT	n.a.
43. WEATHERSTRIPPING, SHADES & BLINDS	n.a.
44. MISCELLANEOUS METAL Skylights	7000
45. FENCES & RETAINING WALLS	n.a.
46. FIREPLACE	n.a.
47. SCREENS, WINDOW	n.a.
48. GARAGE DOOR & HARDWARE	n.a.
49. CLEANUP	1000
50. DRAIN TILE	n.a.
51. LANDSCAPING (interior plants)	1900
52. CONCRETE OR ASPHALT PAVING	n.a.
53. WALKS & EXTERIOR STAIRS (BSM tent/LS)	1500
54. INSURANCE, COMP., P.L. & P.D.	500
55. SOCIAL SECURITY & UNEMP. INS.	4400
56. SUPERVISION, GEN. CONTR.	5280
57. SIGNS	800
58. SUBTOTAL	180,590
59. Contingency @ 10%	18,000
60. SUBTOTAL	198,590
61. ARCH. & ENG. FEES	21,800
62. OVERHEAD & PROFIT (10% of #60)	19,800
TOTAL COST	240,190

I certify that the above is, to the best of my knowledge, a true and correct statement of the estimated cost of this work.

Signed: _Rudy Borden_   Date: 9 Dec 81

JAMES R. BORDEN   ARCHITECT C 56

sion, general contractor's estimated profit of $19,800, and a contingency reserve of $18,000 to cover any unforeseen costs.

THE BANK PROPOSES TO KEEP 5 PERCENT

Although our architect included a contingency reserve of $18,000, the bank added an additional 5 percent contingency reserve of $9,580. With the architect and the contractor I arranged that any unused portion of the $18,000 contract contingency reserve would be applied to painting the exterior. I then asked Gillam for the same application of the $9,850 reserve held by the bank.

The banker said that any portion of the contingency reserve not used to pay for scheduled rehabbing would have to be applied as a credit on my account to reduce the amount of the principal.

I said, "That sounds fine, but really isn't fair, as I will not be able to use the money, although I am paying all the costs and fees to process the entire loan, including the contingency reserve."

So Gillam agreed to apply the complete unused portion of the contingency reserve toward painting the exterior, to be designated as "extra work."

Neither contract nor bank reserve had to be drawn on to pay for scheduled work, showing the thoroughness of our contract. We applied the entire $27,580 toward painting all of the exterior at a total cost of $38,000. The remaining cost of $10,420 for painting was paid from net income.

ESCROW STATEMENT

Surprises may occur when you receive an escrow statement covering a bank loan, or any loan for that matter. Following is the specific statement applying to the Bank of America arrangements for funding of La Peralta rehabbing.

Title Policy Fees (guaranteeing title)	$1,223.60
Recording fees	8.00

Check to Builder's Control (to make disbursements)

Principal Amount	230,326.93
Contingency reserve (bank must okay payout)	9,580.00
Builder's control fee (inspection and auditing)	3,454.88

Escrow fees (drawing papers, etc.)   125.00

Loan origination fee (Bank of America loan fee)   10,391.74

Appraisal fee (Bank of America appraisal before and after)   1,080.00
($290.00 prepaid deposit)

Tax lien service (notice to bank if future taxes unpaid)   16.50

Architect fee (to William and Lucille Nickerson to pay direct to architect for past plans and ongoing supervision)   21,000.00

Net proceeds reconciliation (check to Nickersons)   198.35

Total amount of loan $277,405.00

The loan pays out in fifteen years at $3,384.35 monthly, including 12¼ percent interest. The 2 percent saving below the market in interest represents a total saving of approximately $41,611 over the fifteen-year life of the loan.

UNEXPECTED PROFIT FROM SHORT-TERM INVESTMENT

With a standard construction loan the funds are usually advanced by the lender in "progress payments" as needed to pay for work as it progresses. The borrower is then charged for interest in stages as the funds are credited to his account for disbursement.

Banker Gillam explained that the regular procedure with funds from tax-free municipal bonds was to deposit all the committed funds, except for the bank's charges and reserve, with Builder's Control as soon as the necessary paperwork was completed. Builder's Control was an organization established to receive loan funds in trust, audit all authorized invoices and statements, then disburse all construction-loan payments.

This procedure meant paying interest on all the loan money even though it would only be needed to make progress payments over the expected completion time of six months.

I asked my contact at Builder's Control if it was possible to invest the funds until needed. It developed that this was permissible, provided that it was deposited in a secure and readily available account, like a bank savings account. I authorized investing most of the funds in thirty-day time certificates, which were paying 14 percent interest. Then Builder's Control could draw the money monthly as needed to pay bills.

Instead of losing money by paying 12¼ percent for idle funds, I was actually making a profit of 1¾ percent. The total bonus interest that I received from this ploy was slightly over $8,000.

UNCLE SAM WANTS TO PAY YOU MORE FOR REHABBING

Tax laws keep changing, but at this writing in 1986 a major improvement project like the rehab work at La Peralta generally qualifies for the eighteen-year Accelerated Cost Recovery System (ACRS) depreciation schedule. Also, rehabbers of qualified low-income housing can write off all capital expenditures, up to $40,000 per unit, in five years.

In addition to depreciation allowances and subsidized interest previously described, Uncle Sam will pay you investment credits against other tax liabilities "where there has been a substantial rehabilitation. The rehabilitation expenditures during the 24-month period that ends on the last day of your tax year are more than the greater of (1) $5,000, or (2) your adjusted basis in the building."

Rehab investment credits against taxes apply to older rehabilitated buildings and Certified Historic Structures, with the following percentages, pertaining to overall rehab costs: 15 percent for buildings at least thirty years old; 20 percent for buildings at least forty years old; and 25 percent for Certified Historic Structures listed on the National Parks and Recreation Department Register or within an area designed as a Historic District. Many buildings are being added to the official list after the owner files the department's printed application.

According to IRS Publication 572, Investment Credit, "You can take an investment credit for the rehabiliation or reconstruction of older buildings used for nonresidential purposes and for certified historic structures used for both residential rental and nonresidential purposes if the property is recovery property.

"A qualified rehabilitated building is *any* building (including its structural components) that meets the following requirements: (1) The building must be substantially rehabilitated; (2) The building must be placed in service before the beginning of the rehabilitation; (3) No more than 25% of the existing external walls of the building can be replaced during the rehabilitation."

A WARNING AND AN INVITATION

At this writing, except for certified Historic Structures, rehab credits do not apply to apartments, but to buildings for nonresidential use, like commercial rentals. Does this mean you cannot qualify for rehab credits if you own an apartment house? Not necessarily. You can apply for recognition as a certified Historic Structure. Or you can still take the credit if your total rehab expenditures for nonresidential use exceed your adjusted basis in the building.

Your adjusted basis is your building cost, exclusive of land and personal property, less depreciation. This calculation can make your adjusted basis quite low if you have taken depreciation for several years. I traded for La Peralta in 1967. All the depreciation since then made the adjusted basis of my building considerably lower than my commercial rehab expenditures. This qualified me for the 20 percent rehab credit, since La Peralta was erected in 1908, as mentioned.

If you decide to consider a rehabbing project, current details as to applicable depreciation and credits should be reviewed with your accountant, as tax laws keep changing.

As described in this and other chapters, the realistic application of costs in figuring my $2-for-$1 formula envisages out-of-pocket costs, which can be substantially influenced by tax credits and deductions. You should earn a minimum value of $2 for every $1 of net cost.

Bringing dead space to life as at La Peralta, so that a maintenance drawback becomes a profitable income attraction, is one example of thousands of conversions, rehabilitations, and modernizations in downtown older-building areas throughout the United States. The next chapter will cite other specific examples covering major metropolitan areas nationwide.

CHAPTER 9

Real Estate Gold Mines in the Heart of the City

UNTIL RECENTLY, THE bulldozer and wrecking ball have relentlessly destroyed the proud downtown buildings that had been allowed to decay in our richest urban areas. The movement from town to country cost city businesses untold fortunes, as spacious new malls drew shoppers and small businesses to the suburbs.

In recent years, though, the trend has dramatically reversed, and the city has again become the magnetic pole that attracts new businesses and new opportunities. Once-scorned edifices, from Victorian single-family homes to stately apartment and office buildings, are again recognized as valuable historic assets that can and should be preserved. And all of these once-proud properties are rich with possibility for fixer-upper real estate investors of all levels.

This dramatic turn of the tide in the fortunes of our cities has been encouraged by significant mortgage incentives, like 5-percent-down financing and tax credits sponsored by national, state, and city governments. Cities spur their own growth by offering five-to-ten-year property tax abatements and other rehabilitation encouragements. Jersey City, for example, offers 95 percent financing to buy and fix up a fourplex like Wildwood, as long as the investor or an immediate family member lives in

one of the units. As a result of urban rehabilitation encouragement, as much money is now being spent to transform and rehab
old buildings as for new construction.

A NATIONWIDE TREND

The swelling national trend toward rebuilding the heart of the
city can be observed in every metropolitan area. In recognition
of the mushrooming interest and growing need, courses on preservation and rehabilitation of existing structures are taught in
about eighty colleges and universities.

Costs of all types of rehabilitation, including conversion and
modernization, approximate half the cost of new construction,
developing income at half the cost. Each $1 spent for rehabbing
adds to the national economy a value of at least $2, a far-reaching
echo of my two-for-one theory.

From Boston to San Francisco, from New York to Los Angeles,
in downtown and close-in areas, individuals like the Wrights and
groups of investors have rehabilitated many thousands of single-
family homes, duplexes, and fourplexes. They have installed
modern conveniences, like central heat and air conditioning, and
preserved artful, previously belittled Victorian construction details, like intricate gingerbread trim and dormer and bay windows.

Thousands of decrepit buildings, large and small, have been
rehabilitated for similar use, such as housing. Many have been
converted to new usage, some from housing to commercial and
some from commercial to housing.

MANY BEGINNERS START WITH AN OLD INNER-CITY MANSION

Elegant Victorian homes are sprawled like sleeping white ele-
phants across the country, needing only a little prodding to be
wakened and put to work. An easy transformation for either a

beginner or an expert is from a many-roomed single-family home to a rooming house, a conversion that takes little more than paint, a spruced-up yard, and the addition of a couple of baths.

You might multiply the potential income from a standard monthly-rental rooming house by choosing either of two alternatives, depending on location and costs of conversion.

1. You might be able to install small efficiency kitchens at nominal cost and convert the sleeping rooms into apartments at three or four times the present rental value.

2. You might find that it pays to convert to transient rentals with the further attraction of using the big main kitchen for serving breakfast, thereby joining the rapidly spreading ranks of potentially quite profitable bed-and-breakfast inns.

After you gain experience with converting a home, either of these two alternatives might be applied to an old fleabag flophouse hotel in the heart of the inner city. You could convert to kitchenette apartments or to bed-and-breakfast transient rentals, with further alternatives of converting the ground floor to commercial rentals, the basement to coin-laundry and mini-storage units, and the attic to rooms or apartments.

Yet another trend in the inner city is to renovate a fine old residence into a duplex, with one half for income and the other owner occupied. This is very common in New York, San Francisco, Boston, Baltimore and elsewhere.

BE OPEN-MINDED AND BE WILLING TO TAKE A NEW LOOK

Commercial realtors used to say, "Don't mix commercial and residential rentals in the same building. Operate either one or the other."

Conrad Hilton was widely criticized for money-grubbing when he converted just about every available inch of showy and cavernous lobbies to retail rentals.

Now as costs of land and construction keep spiraling upward, the trend of renting most nonproductive lobby and dead-storage space in basements and attics is commonly accepted.

IMPROVEMENT IS A NEVER-ENDING PROCESS

When you complete building plans after myriad recommendations from architects, contractors, and other owners, you begin to think that at last you have arrived at ultimate conclusions that will result in a 100 percent satisfactory structure. That is what I thought after completing my first new construction. The plans incorporated all the knowledge and advice that my wife and I could gather, plus our own best judgment at the time.

As soon as the edifice was finished, Lucille and I saw scads of areas where we could have done better by making other choices. And we have never yet seen a brand-new building that could not stand some improvement as soon as it was finished, be it for housing, offices, stores, or other use.

Even minor improvements can take months to finish, and by the time a project is completed there can be new and improved ways of tackling the same problems, sometimes at great savings in energy and cost. Tastes and preferences change in a short space of time, and a state-of-the-art architectural change can be yesterday's news by the time the alterations are completed. Solar panels can always be added to a roof, a hot tub will always be welcomed in the atrium, and additional parking spaces (for cars, boats, or recreational vehicles) will almost always be put to good use.

A 1984 survey by *Buildings Magazine* indicates that 90 percent of the nation's building owners and managers are continually modernizing and remodeling, and 29 percent of the modernized buildings were less than ten years old. The biggest category affected buildings ten to twenty years old, constituting 35.6 percent of all modernization projects.

All structures at all times can stand some improvement. Anything that you can think of that could go into a building can be improved. As a founding director of Carmel Valley Manor, a Congregationalist-sponsored retirement home, I had a voice in choosing as our architects one of the most prestigious firms in the country, Skidmore, Owings and Merrill. Despite the firm's experience and outstanding accomplishments, many changes were necessary both during and after construction.

OLDSTERS NEED MORE MENDING

Upon completion of any major renovation or remodeling job, most people recognize a dozen ways they could have done things better. Even the smallest fixer-upper investor can learn from the experience of the big boys in the rehabilitation field. Witness the historic and elegant Hotel del Coronado, across the bay from San Diego. Opened in 1888 as one of the world's largest wooden structures, according to *Buildings Magazine,* it has been completely renovated at least four times in the last twenty years.

Among close to ten thousand restored historic properties across the country, other revered downtown hotels undergoing major rehabilitation include, with their rehab costs:

- $90 million for the U. S. Grant Hotel, San Diego, California, built in 1910 by the general's son
- $65 million for the Mayflower Hotel, Washington, D.C., built in 1925
- $55 million for the Four Seasons Olympic Hotel, Seattle, Washington, built in 1924
- $38 million for the Clarion Hotel, New Orleans, Louisiana, built in 1925 as the Jung Hotel
- $25 million for the Peabody Hotel, Memphis, Tennessee, built in 1869
- $22 million for the St. Anthony Intercontinental Hotel, San Antonio, Texas, built in 1909
- $16 million for the Heathman Hotel, Portland, Oregon, built in 1927.

Revitalizing of downtown areas by rehabbing of spectacular city landmarks encourages the rehabbing of adjacent homes and apartments and also encourages major new and rebuilt inner-city shopping centers and malls, and these are springing up all over the country.

The older a building, the more continuing rehabilitation it will need. And where do you find the potentially profitable older structures? They are planted smack in the heart of the city because they got first choice of the most desirable locations. There is a tremendous surge to congregate in city centers and fix up these aging buildings.

Old folks vie with young folks to lead the way toward living in the previously shunned heart of the city. The mushrooming ranks of young and old combine younger, high-income single tenants and wealthier senior citizens who have sold their empty suburban nests. Both want to shorten or avoid commuting traffic, not only to be closer to work, but to enjoy inner-city amenities like movies, plays, symphonies, athletic contests, opera, and ballet. All the attractions help to swell the growing numbers who crave convenient in-town housing. And each year a person ages increases his or her desire to be close to doctors' offices, hospitals, clinics, and other health facilities.

SAN FRANCISCO LEADS THE WAY BACK TO THE CITY

Trend-leading San Francisco exemplifies the gathering momentum that is sweeping the nation back to Metropole, past the suburbs into the very heart of the city, counteracting the previous exodus. To quote *U.S. News & World Report* under its heading "Downs and Ups," "The population of San Francisco hit a peak of 775,000 right after World War II and then went into a slow but steady decline that continued until 1980. Between 1970 and 1980, it dropped to 678,974—but in recent years some 5,000 new residents have been moving in every six months. The population, now at 705,700, is youthful and well-to-do. Median income is about $30,000 and median age is 34.1."

The same magazine mentions that Victorian homes throughout

the city have been revitalized, "giving the areas much-needed facelifts but tripling prices." In many areas facelifting of older buildings has tripled and quadrupled values.

COAST TO COAST

San Francisco on the Pacific Coast participates in the cityward trend of the pace-setting state of California. The most populous state at 25 million people, with 20 percent of the yearly United States increase, it is the most heavily urbanized state in the country. A whopping 91 percent of its citizens live in cities. The nation's cities may seesaw upward and downward like San Francisco in total population growth, but on an overall basis will emulate the cities of California, spurred by a healthy regrowth in a myriad of city amenities.

The growth of the cities creates a continuing demand for more close-in office buildings, shopping centers, and livable housing. In the long run, downtown property can be fixed up by private enterprise to beautify the city and return a good profit. Neglected slum areas that used to be shunned, especially when deteriorating under public ownership, can draw responsible, rent-paying tenants when they are rehabilitated with necessary repairs and desirable improvements.

The answer to obtaining improved housing on a large scale is not public ownership, but a sustained public inducement of private ownership through tax incentives and programs to keep financing and construction costs at reasonable levels.

NEW YORK BOARDS THE BANDWAGON

Across the continent on the Atlantic Coast, New York City has boarded the bandwagon of encouraging city regrowth by sponsoring big redevelopment projects. Witness the $1.6 billion renovation of fabled Times Square, sponsored by both New York City's Public Development Corporation and New York State's

Urban Development Corporation, in conjunction with private-enterprise Park Tower Realty.

Besides considerable rehabilitation of hotels, office buildings, and theaters, new construction involves several modern office buildings, hotels, and special-purpose structures. Included are the fifty-story Marriott Marquis Hotel with 1,876 oversized guest rooms, a 2.4-million-square-foot Merchandise and Apparel Mart, and a 1.8-million-square-foot Convention Center.

Buildings Magazine quotes Anthony Gliedman, commissioner of the Department of Housing Preservation and Development of the City of New York, as stating that our biggest city has reversed from abandoning properties in the 1960s and 1970s to actually gaining housing units in the last six years. In 1977 the number of apartments rehabilitated n New York City was 1,700. In 1983, rehabbed dwellings climbed to 20,000, nearly twelve times as many per year, aided by more encouragement from City Hall and attractive bank programs for financing rehabilitation.

It should be mentioned that swelling city growth has been stimulated by immigration from abroad. Where a major share of immigrants used to head for our farms, a good portion now move to our cities. As an example, one-fourth of all La Peralta tenants in 1986 are immigrants.

REDEVELOPMENT IS SPRINGING OUT ALL OVER!

Nearly every major city, from Boston and New York to Chicago and St. Louis, and on to Los Angeles and San Francisco, is sponsoring redevelopment projects. Name almost any city and you will find ongoing redevelopment.

Three outstanding examples to combat economic decay and turn the population tide inward towards the heart of the city are Detroit's aptly named Renaissance Center, the St. Louis Union Station Restoration, and Baltimore's Inner Harbor Development. Baltimore retored blocks of old, run-down buildings by selling them to fixer-upper owners for $1. Over ten-thousand dwelling units within ten minutes of the center of Baltimore have been rehabbed in the past ten years.

QUICK FIXER-UPPERS

Fixing up older buildings is the quickest way to obtain demanded housing at comparatively reasonable cost. Housing ranks second in all metropolitan rehab efforts throughout the country, with office buildings number one. Rehabbing covers modernization in the same field, like fixing up older apartments into more convenient and attractive housing. Rehabbing also includes a great deal of conversion of use, like changing abandoned warehouses, railway stations, and schools into apartments, offices, retail stores, and hotels and motels.

To help give you ideas on what you might consider for purchase and rehabbing in all sizes from single-family homes to hundred-and thousand-unit rentals, I will cite specific areas from the Atlantic to the Pacific.

SHIPYARD CONVERTED INTO HOUSING AND COMMERCIAL

A narrow estuary divides the Eastbay cities of Oakland and Alameda. Across the estuary from La Peralta, we can see from our rooftop the decaying 206-acre Bethlehem Shipyards, which have stayed vacant for thirty-five years. I am quite familiar with Bethlehem's layout, as I used to engineer its telephone services as a representative of Pacific Bell.

Since 1977, Alameda Marina Village Associates has been converting the associated shipyards and steel mill into desirable housing, office, and retail space, featuring marina apartments with boat slips. The $200 million Marina Village multi-use project is expected to take until 1990 to complete. Because the brick powerhouse and 85-foot-high-by-552-foot-long Bethlehem Building are listed on the National Register for Historic Places, the developers earn the maximum 25 percent federal investment tax credit for their conversion.

PENCIL FACTORY CONVERTED INTO APARTMENTS

The Bethlehem steel mill produced massive steel plates for construction projects like the Golden Gate Bridge and Hoover Dam. On a somewhat smaller production scale in the Eastbay area, an Oakland pencil manufacturer also went out of business. His vacated building, which I bought, remodeled, and sold, was converted into forty desirable apartments.

NATIONWIDE EXAMPLES

In the field of real estate there are two interesting and highly educational monthly magazines that I read regularly. They are *Buildings,* published by Stamats Communications, Inc., and subtitled *The Facilities Construction and Management Magazine,* and *Professional Builder, Apartment Business,* published by Cahners Publishing Co. and subtitled *The Magazine of Housing and Light Construction.*

Both monthlies have printed scores of detailed articles covering rehab projects nationwide. *Buildings* editor Craig A. Henrich and *Professional Builder* editor Roy L. Diez have kindly given me permission to cite a number of outstanding examples from their magazines, as I will indicate below.

CONVERTING FOUR TRANSIENT HOTELS TO LEASED APARTMENTS

One of many profitable conversions is from run-down older downtown hotels to senior-citizen-oriented apartments. The leases are semipermanent, as most qualified tenants move in with the expectation of remaining indefinitely.

Four examples are the block-square sixty-year-old Hotel Oakland, one block from my La Peralta Apartments, converted into 315 apartments; the Commonwealth Hotel, a similar conversion in downtown Chicago, where 200 hotel rooms were converted to 150 apartments (*Buildings*); the 602-unit Jefferson Arms Apartments in downtown St. Louis, converted from 850 hotel rooms built for the World's Fair in 1904 (*Professional Builder*); and the sixty-eight-year-old Envoy Towers, a former leading hotel in Washington, D.C., converted into 302 apartments (*Buildings*).

In all four conversions, many of the original sleeping rooms, as at La Peralta, were big enough to convert to studio and one-bedroom apartments by adding a compact kitchen. This money-maker is often used to transform a large old house into apartments. In other cases two smaller rooms were joined into one apartment in order to have sufficient space for a kitchen installation. Commercial and retail spaces, such as small stores and offices, were also added on the ground floors.

THREE VACANT PUBLIC STRUCTURES TRANSFORMED INTO ATTRACTIVE APARTMENTS

Three rehab examples on the East Coast involved converting a city hall and two schoolhouses into attractive apartments. In Harrisburg, Pennsylvania, the old City Hall was converted to twenty desirable apartments (*Professional Builder*). In the same city the obsolete Edison School, built in 1918, was converted into 125 modern apartments, catering to elderly, handicapped, and low-income families (*Buildings*).

The Fox School in Hartford, Connecticut, was also converted into apartments, ninety attractive units for senior-citizen housing (*Buildings*).

GENERAL MOTORS HELPS UPDATE 125 DETROIT HOMES

Most new real estate investors, like the Wrights, start out by fixing up a single-family home. Such individual owner-rehabbers spent over $40 billion in 1985 for rehabbing homes.

Updating a single-family home is a rewarding fixer-upper project any beginning investor can tackle with the expectation of making high and sound profits. Some owners tackle one home at a time. Others contract to improve several at the same time.

One massive eighteen-block updating project involving 125 single-family homes was New Center Commons, sponsored by General Motors with fourteen limited partners, near GM's world headquarters (*Professional Builder*). Most of the rehabbing of the approximately eighty-year-old structures involved renovation of existing features like wood and brick trim on the exteriors and interiors, including restored fireplaces. About the only clear-cut replacement modernization was more up-to-date kitchens, which were equipped with modern appliances and increased cabinets to provide ample storage.

New Center Commons is a completely self-contained city area within the city of Detroit. General Motors expressed a desire to make the surrounding area more attractive, and, incidentally, to make the project pay for itself.

THREE LODGE HALLS INTO INCOME PROPERTY

As lodge membership dwindles or lodges move, many cities witness transitions from lodge buildings to apartments, condominiums, offices, or other income-property use.

The sixty-year-old Knights of Pythias headquarters in New York City lay vacant for close to twenty years. The city took possession and utilized the building in 1974 for its City University classrooms. But the city again abandoned this awkward conversion. In 1980, imaginative developers, the Columbus 70 Group, acquired the property and converted it to eighty-three fairly large, desirable apartments, which they sold as condominiums (*Buildings*).

Two further examples of lodge conversions are the sixty-year-old Moose Club Building, a block from my La Peralta Apartments in Oakland, California; and the sixty-year-old Elks Club Building in Wichita, Kansas (*Buildings*).

NEW YORK PARKING GARAGE INTO CONDO APARTMENTS

New York developer Jerry Katz transformed a fifty-year-old parking garage, formerly used by the Hoboken Ferry and Hudson River Steamboats, into eighty-four attractive apartments that readily sold as condominiums (*Buildings*). Condos enjoy a continuing national marketability, spreading across the country between the two condominium centers of New York City and Hawaii.

SCOTTSDALE INN INTO CONDO APARTMENTS

Donald Kellogg built a mansion on a twenty-acre site in Scottsdale, Arizona, in the 1930s, and it was turned into the Casa Blanca Inn in the 1940s. Many owners feel they are doing well to transform an old mansion into a fourplex. But developer Alan Mishkin decided to convert the inn into 129 saleable luxury condominiums, following the ongoing trend of condominium sales that started in Hawaii in the 1950s and caught on in other resort areas from mountains to beaches (*Professional Builder*)

HOUSTON FLEABAG INTO LUXURY HOTEL

An example of modernizing for the same basically transient housing use, minus bedbugs, was the transformation of the run-down sixty-year-old, 165-room Auditorium Hotel into the luxurious eighty-five-unit Lancaster Hotel (*Buildings*). As a Historic Landmark, the conversion qualified for both the federal 25 percent investment credit and a property-tax reduction granted by the city of Houston.

CHICAGO STORE INTO UNIVERSITY USE

DePaul University bought Lyon & Healy's sixty-five-year-old music store in the heart of downtown Chicago and converted it into the school's administrative offices and computer sciences department in its College of Commerce *(Buildings)*.

FLORIDA HOTEL ANNEX GOES INTO COLLEGE

Another conversion for educational purposes was the transformation of a hotel annex in St. Augustine into Flagler College's Kenan Hall, encompassing various educational usages, including classrooms, offices, and another computer science laboratory (*Buildings*).

REHABBING THE HEART OF CHICAGO

Chicago investors Murdoch & Coll have concentrated their efforts on rehabbing several older, neglected commercial buildings in the downtown Loop area. Profitable examples include the seventy-year-old, twenty-story Fisher Building and the fifty-year-old, forty-five-story Randolph Tower, which was originally built as the Steuben Building (*Buildings*).

Another downtown Chicago rehabilitation involved the hundred-year-old, seventeen-story Old Colony Building, completely renovated by the Old Colony Limited Partnership (*Buildings*).

VACANT LOWELL MILL INTO RENTABLE OFFICES

Developers Malcolm F. Fryer, Jr., and Richard E. Dobroth completely rehabbed the vacant 121-year-old Wannalancit Textile Mill in Lowell, Massachusetts, into readily rentable offices and a high-technology center (*Buildings*).

PHILADELPHIA MEN'S STORE TRANSFORMS INTO BANK

The building that housed John Wanamaker Men's Store, a leading establishment in the heart of Philadelphia since it opened in the 1930s, resurfaced in a remarkable rehabilitation as the main office of the Philadelphia National Bank (*Buildings*).

ALABAMA RAILWAY DEPOT CHUGS INTO BIG MONEY

With slackened use, railway depots are often abandoned. They are usually located in the highly sought-after downtown heart of a city, where rehabbing pays big money through transformation. A good example is the eighteen-story Bank for Savings Building in Birmingham, Alabama, converted from an obsolete Union Passenger Depot by Hexalon Real Estate, Inc. (*Buildings*).

CONVERTING AN EIGHTY-YEAR-OLD BOSTON WAREHOUSE

The Atlantic Building, a five-story warehouse on the Boston waterfront designed in 1899, was converted to six rentable stories, with five stories of desirable offices and the first story leased for retail and restaurant use (*Buildings*). The Northland Investment Company paid about $3.2 million for the property in 1982, and spent $6.5 million for rehabilitation. The 1984 estimated value of the modernized building was approximately $15 million. This was a typical and not unusual increase in value of less than $2 for $1 in total costs, but more than $2 for each $1 spent on rehabbing.

RICHMOND'S GOTHIC CITY HALL INTO OFFICES

The ninety-year-old Richmond, Virginia, City Hall was scheduled for demolition when the Historic Society of Richmond came to the rescue of the High Victorian Gothic structure and spearheaded its transformation into a desirable office building (*Buildings*). Because the building is listed on the National Register, its owners, Old City Hall Associates, received an encouraging 25 percent federal investment tax credit.

BIG APPLE REHABS OF YOUNG AND OLD BUILDINGS

An outstanding Park Avenue, New York City, rehab involved the 1.5-million-square-foot, fifty-story World Headquarters, Manufacturers Hanover Trust Plaza (*Buildings*). It was well built in the 1960s, but was already in need of modernization in order to meet requirements for electronic equipment and energy conservation. This exemplifies my conclusion that all construction can stand some improvement as soon as it is built; in only twenty years this facility was in need of major rehabilitation.

A remodernization of an older ten-story building at 122 Fifth Avenue was encouraged by a 20 percent federal investment tax credit (*Buildings*). This was available because the building was constructed at the turn of the century and qualified for maximum tax credit (available for buildings at least forty years old). Another example of a continuing need for improvement, this building was modernized in the 1950s. Included was a cover-up of the then old-fashioned but originally beautiful moldings, marble columns, and granite, marble, and limestone facade. The remodernization followed the trend to remove previous cover-ups and feature original surfaces and details.

NEW YORK'S PARK AVENUE ATRIUM THE BIGGEST REHAB

Over 60 percent of the readers of *Buildings* magazine, including major contractors, concentrate their commercial rehabilitation work on modernizing and remodeling office buildings. An outstanding commercial example is the Park Avenue Atrium, New York City's largest rehabilitation project, covering an entire city block near Grand Central Terminal, in the heart of the city (*Buildings*).

Owners Olympia & York completely transformed the sixty-five-year-old Railroad Mail Service Building into twenty-three floors of highly desirable commercial space, combining three floors of retail space topped by twenty floors of offices.

OVERALL REASONS FOR MODERNIZATION

As in all real estate investments, the overall objective for rehabbing, whether modernizing or converting, is to produce the highest-paying use at the least proportionate cost.

The following specific reasons for modernization, including remodeling, were given by building owners and managers in a 1984 survey by *Buildings* magazine:

- To keep up with continued expansion of the organization, as well as to bring the buildings up to the standard of those constructed within the last one to three years
- To maintain buildings and receive the highest possible rental income
- To provide added demand activity capability to existing electric load management system allowing better control demand (Increase electric capacity)
- To remain competitive with other office buildings in the area

- To modernize the shopping center to offer a more competitive product in the local market area (Meet competition)
- To consolidate major departments between two buildings
- To bring the HVAC (heating, venting, air-conditioning) systems of some very old apartments into more efficient status
- To improve lighting levels and use up-to-date color schemes
- To lower costs/expenses, especially of utilities
- To bring the facilities as close as possible back to an original (or better) usefulness
- To keep all projects leased due to a soft market with high vacancies

APPLY ALL POSSIBLE EXPENSES TO REHABBING

When rehabilitation qualifies for tax credits, a beneficial accounting strategy is to allocate to the rehab project as many related expenses as possible. This includes items like painting that could be expensed entirely in one year, but produce maximum tax savings in the long run if they are added to rehab credits and depreciated. Remember that a credit is a 100 percent reduction of income taxes. A deduction for repairs, depreciation, or other expenses can amount to no more than a 50 percent reduction of income taxes, and that much only in the highest tax bracket.

MORE ABOUT BENEFITS

Rehabilitation can greatly increase gross rental income. Significant tax credits and accelerated depreciation can swell the amount of net bankable income. Another plus on a thorough rehab job is the possibility of slashing energy costs at least 50 percent by renewal or replacement. At less than half the cost of new construction, the benefits of rehabbing can transform an alligator money-loser into a spectacular money-maker.

Besides the pleasure of earning handsome profits there is a strong feeling of satisfaction in putting your imagination into action, so you can actually prove wrong the sacrosanct saying "You can't make a silk purse out of a sow's ear."

I hope that the many examples cited in this chapter will stir you to investigate some of the countless rehab opportunities.

"POOR MOMMY"

Everybody has his own priorities, and when it comes to rehabilitation you can't please all of the people all of the time. Consider the plight of a neighbor couple who married and bought a two-bedroom house with a two-car garage. When their family swelled to include three little girls, the couple converted the double garage into two more bedrooms, with a bath between.

I asked the family how they liked the new arrangement, and one of the little girls offered an answer I'll never forget. "Us girls like it fine," she piped up. "We each have our own bedroom now. But poor Mommy, she still has to sleep in the same room as Daddy!"

CHAPTER 10

Over a Half Million in Twenty-One Months

MAY 15, 1982, six months after buying the Wildwood fourplex and fourteen months after buying the Spruce Street house, the Wrights analyzed their progress.

Much of the work in his $22,000 contract was accomplished by Jack Armstrong personally, and he was still able to complete all specifications in three months. At their low monthly rent of $275 the four tenants stayed on while the work was underway.

When the improvements and repairs were completed the rents were raised to $495. All tenants moved out within sixty days. Within a month thereafter the Wrights rented to new tenants at $550. Thus the rents paid for loan payments and other expenses.

IN FOURTEEN MONTHS THE WRIGHTS ACCUMULATE $168,578

With rents totaling $2,200 monthly the Wrights figured their resale value at $220,000. The $80,000 first mortgage balance was paid down to $78,680, leaving a net Wildwood equity of $141,320.

The Wrights could have financed their improvements in many

ways, including an easily obtainable improvement loan. But they chose to pay cash from their money market account. Their remaining money market balance now came to $23,844, including $1,135 for six months' interest.

Their credit union balance, including six months' additional deposits of $200 and $54 interest, came to $3,414. This brought their total cash in the two savings accounts to $27,258.

Adding the Wildwood net equity of $141,320 to the $27,258 in savings gave the Wrights a net worth after fourteen months of investment of $168,578, surpassing the three-year goal of $147,959 suggested in Chapter 3.

READY TO MOVE UP A DIGIT

"It looks like we're ready to move up to two-digit properties," said Norman Wright to his wife. "Something above ten units."

"With our successful experiences," said Karen, "we might even go three digits, to one hundred or more units."

"We certainly can. If we can work out the financing we might take on a hundred apartments sooner than we think. But I'd feel more comfortable with our next move if we found a good buy somewhere between our fourplex and fifty units."

"I would, too. We can be open-minded as to size, but concentrate somewhere in between ten and fifty units."

"In the meantime," suggested Norman, "let's just sit on Wildwood instead of trying to sell. Maybe we can trade it for something bigger."

"Especially now that Wildwood is in good shape," agreed Karen. "I'm anxious to start shopping for another property like Spruce Street and Wildwood that really needs improvement, something that looks bad but has basically sound construction."

"And can be bought at a bargain," added Norman.

The Wrights answered for-sale ads in the *Metropole News*. They also advised previously contacted realtors that they were in the market for another "Nickerson Deal." Included were Patti Arthur, who had sold them Spruce Street, and Cindy Seekum, who had sold them Wildwood. Cindy Seekum had learned she would have to extend herself to satisfy the hard-bargaining Wrights, but she knew her firm could earn many future commissions by cooperating with such canny investors.

CITY HALL SAYS KNOCK PARADISE DOWN

The Wrights were driving through a downtown Metropole area to meet a realtor at a prospective property. They noticed several people crowded around a man nailing a notice to the front door of a dilapidated-looking three-story apartment house. Above the door was a crudely hand-carved wooden sign:

The Wrights stopped to investigate and saw that the cardboard notice read:

NOTICE TO VACATE

THIS BUILDING IS UNINHABITABLE

All tenants are ordered to vacate at once. This building to be demolished unless it meets city Codes within 30 days.

DATED June 18, 1982
City of Metropole
Building Department
CITY HALL

The man had finished nailing up the notice on the front door and proceeded to the back door, where he was nailing up a duplicate notice.

The Wrights asked him, "Why are you posting these notices?"

"I don't know anything about it, except I got orders to post them. Anybody that wants any information can see the Building Department at City Hall."

A stout, ruddy-faced woman among the spectators told the Wrights, "if you're looking for an apartment, I'm the manager. But I can't rent to nobody with those signs up."

"Actually, we're looking for an apartment house that needs a little fixing up that we can buy," said Karen. "Maybe we're too late, with these notices posted, to do anything with this place."

"We would like to check into it if you could give us the owner's name," said Norman. "I am Norman Wright and this is my wife, Karen. And what is your name?"

"I'm Althea Magli. The owner's name is Bludden, and he's a penny-pinching widower. The city has ordered him many times to fix up the place. There's plumbing repairs and bad wiring needs to be taken care of. The tenants have kicked holes in the plaster walls in most of the apartments. They all need patching and painting. Mr. Bludden keeps telling City Hall to go to hell. He says the tenants done the damage and let them fix it up. So the tenants keep moving out. I got eighteen apartments and half of them are vacant.

"One of the apartments is all burned out and black as coal. The tenant got drunk and fell asleep while he was smoking in bed. He and his roommate girlfriend are both in the hospital. The apartment is all gutted to hell. With all the other things that's gone wrong here, I bet the fire is what triggered City Hall to put up these vacate notices."

Karen asked Mrs. Magli, "How many bedrooms do the apartments have?"

"They all have two bedrooms."

"And what do they usually rent for?"

"$135 unfurnished. And the tenants pay all utilities except water." Mrs. Magli gave Bludden's phone number and address to the Wrights.

THE FLAG OF DISTRESS MEANS "OPPORTUNITY KNOCKS"

Driving to meet Bludden, Norman said, "Nickerson keeps saying that the best buys are in downtown distress properties. We certainly found one, with City Hall threatening to bulldoze it down!"

"It sure looks sufficiently distressful to qualify as a fixer-upper Nickerson Deal," said Karen. "Could be a real money-making sleeper."

When the Wrights met Bludden, Norman said, "We saw the man putting up the City Hall notice that your apartments will be demolished if you don't meet City codes in thirty days. That looks like an impossible order, and you'll lose your building if you don't do anything. We're willing to take the property off your hands and fix up all eighteen apartments to satisfy City Hall. What's the best deal you can give us?"

"If I can get out from under those City Hall highbinders I'm willing to practically give you my property. I'll sell you my equity for $5,000 cash."

"What is the loan?" asked Karen.

"The loan was $180,000 from the Capitol Bank, and it's paid down to about $160,000. The payment is $1,500 a month, including 8 percent interest. That's a mighty good loan these days."

"Is it assumable?" asked Norman.

A $12,000 INSURANCE CHECK SWEETENS THE DEAL

"I don't think you'd have any trouble taking it over as long as you're going to fix up the building," Bludden said. "There is one other thing you have to agree to, though. The insurance company's contractor estimates it would cost $12,000 to repair that burned-up apartment. The insurance company is about to give me a check for that amount, made out to me and their contractor, so I'm supposed to give it to him when he finishes the work. I would expect to keep that $12,000 insurance money. Then you can have a cheaper contractor do the work for a lot less."

"If we have to do the repair work and pay for it, we should get the insurance money," said Karen.

"Well, I'd have to get the insurance check if I'm going to give you such a good deal," said Bludden. "Unless you want to take it and repay me for the $12,000 check plus the $5,000 cash you have to pay me."

"We can talk more about that later," said Norman. "We first have to contact City Hall and verify what needs to be done. Next we have to find out what it costs to fix up the property to satisfy City Hall. Then we have to figure out how to pay for all the repair and improvement work. We'll get back to you as soon as we can."

"Don't delay," warned Bludden. "Or else I'll lose the building and you'll lose a giveaway bargain."

CITY HALL LISTENS TO REASON

The Wrights contacted the Building Department inspector, Mr. Forthy, at City Hall. Norman said, "The Bludden apartments look hopeless. If you tear them down they will come off the tax rolls, of course. My wife and I are willing to take the responsibility of fixing them up if you can cooperate with us and relax some of your requirements.

"We know that Mr. Bludden has been a pain in the neck to you, but all you have asked him to do is impossible. It just wouldn't pay to bring all eighteen apartments up to city codes. If you could be a little more resonable, we could assure you that everything will be taken care of in good order, and the city would continue to collect taxes on the apartments."

Karen said, "We have two good examples of the kind of rehab work we do. A house on Spruce Street and a fourplex on Wildwood Avenue were in about as bad a condition as the Paradise Apartments. You should see them now. They look like new. And that's how the Paradise will look when we get through fixing it up."

City Inspector Forthy said, "I'll look your two projects over to see what kind of repair work you do. You have to understand that a lot of the repair work we told Bludden to do is absolutely necessary. We are very concerned with safety, but I'll consider whether it would be safe to drop some of the code work. Then I'll see if I can get my supervisor's approval. Frankly, there are too many owners like Bludden who want to bleed property, and we react by getting tough with them when we have a chance. My supervisor and I and most of our associates like to encourage fixer-upper owners like yourselves who want to improve property."

After checking Spruce Street and Wildwood and talking with his supervisor, Inspector Forthy agreed in writing to a considerably trimmed list of requirements. He included a proviso that everything had to be taken care of within six months, and also provided that the fire-damaged apartment would be completely repaired and brought up to current city codes within sixty days. Forthy agreed that the Wrights could rent each vacant apartment as soon as it passed inspection, rather than have to wait until the entire rehab project was completed.

THE BUYERS TAKE OVER, JULY 10, 1982, WITH NO MONEY DOWN, AND POCKET $2,000

The Wrights advised Bludden of all city requirements, including the most urgent demand—"Completely repair the damaged apartment in sixty days, or else the city will order the entire building demolished."

Norman told Bludden, "The other work can wait, but we can't delay fixing up the burned-out apartment. We have to have the $12,000 insurance money to pay for it."

Bludden said, "I'm sure you can get the work done for half as much. I'll compromise and accept half the insurance check, plus the $5,000 cash. That will make $11,000 that I'll get for my equity."

Bludden finally agreed to settle for $10,000 from the insurance proceeds as the entire down payment, so the Wrights would wind up taking over the Paradise Apartments and paying no money down. In fact, they would receive a $2,000 credit from their share of the $12,000 insurance check. The Wrights would be responsible for all needed repairs, including fixing up the fire-damaged apartment.

The Wrights had their attorney draw up an agreement of sale, signed by Norman and Karen and Bludden, calling for a total purchase price of $170,000. The actual cost to the Wrights was $158,000 "as is," as the agreement was subject to depositing the $12,000 insurance check in escrow. $10,000 was to be paid to Bludden from escrow and credited to the Wrights as their down payment, and the Wrights were to receive $2,000 in cash.

The agreement was also prudently subject to the buyers assuming the existing Capitol Bank loan of approximately $160,000, and "subject to the Buyers being able to arrange financing satisfactory to the Buyers to pay for all necessary repairs, for which the Buyers will be completely responsible."

A FAVORABLE CONTRACT

The Wrights obtained estimates from three general contractors. Their bids for identical work were $205,000, $155,000, and $119,000. The highest bidder, the insurance company's contractor, employed all union labor, and the two lower bidders were nonunion. The two higher bidders employed on-the-job foremen. The lowest bidder worked as a foreman and jack-of-all-trades on all his jobs.

The lowest bidder, as expected, was Jack Armstrong, the same general contractor who had handled the Wrights' profitable improvements on the Spruce Street house and the Wildwood fourplex. Although many unimaginative contractors shun improvement work, Armstrong said that he bid low because he loved the challenge of fixing up run down property. Armstrong wrote a contract to take care of all City Hall demands, plus completely painting the exterior and interior, for $119,000.

The contract included an allowance of $6,000 to pay for the repairs to the burned-out apartment, doing the same work that the insurance company's contractor figured at $12,000. The Wrights signed the favorable contract after adding a safety proviso: "This contract subject to the Wrights being able to arrange financing satisfactory to them."

THE IMPERTURBABLE BANK BECOMES ANXIOUS

The bank officers, of course, were anxious to have the Paradise repaired and improved, rather than see a major part of their security demolished. Their real estate vice president, Mr. Yeager, was unusually receptive to the request of the Wrights, who asked for the following:

1. Without penalty, fee, or change of interest rate, the Wrights would continue with the existing first mortgage, payable $1,500 monthly, including 8 percent interest.
2. The bank to advance $119,000 to cover the improvement and repair work.
3. The $119,000 improvement funds to be paid to the contractor in weekly "progress payments" as the work was completed.
4. The $119,000 improvement loan would be secured by a separate second mortgage, payable $1,500 monthly, including 12 percent interest, until paid in full.
5. The first payment on the improvement loan to start forty-five days after the work was completed.

After some discussion Mr. Yeager agreed to the entire proposal with two exceptions. "The minimum loan and appraisal fee I can charge you on an improvement loan is 5 percent. We can just add the $5,950 to your construction cost and make the loan $124,950. Also, your improvement payments can stay at $1,500 monthly, but the loan will have to bear a five-year due date."

The Wrights expected the loan fee, which was not unreasonable. They told Mr. Yeager that they disliked going against my basic advice to avoid potentially dangerous balloon payments, like the balance that would be owing on the $124,950 improvement loan when it would become due in five years.

Mr. Yeager was adamant about both his conditions. "Most loans turn over in five years as a property is either sold or refinanced. Surely you will do one or the other before the five-year due date, which has to be in your loan. I can't change the bank's policy."

The Wrights realized that they had to accept the unwelcome balloon payment or seek other financing. They did not expect to better the Capitol Bank's overall arrangements, so they accepted Mr. Yeager's proposal.

A SWEET AFTERMATH

After completion of the repair and improvement work, the Wrights' total outlay, including the purchase cost, came to $282,950. Five months after the Wrights acquired the Paradise Apartments, all eighteen units were renting at $375 each, totaling $6,750 monthly, establishing a market value of approximately $675,000. This gave the Wrights an estimated profit of $392,050 as recompense for the time and effort they devoted to an apartment house that City Hall was prepared to demolish.

On December 10, 1982, the Wrights figured their financial statement.

Equity in Paradise Apartments   Approximately $393,116

(The rents have paid loan payments, repairs, and other expenses. Five payments on the first mortgage and three payments on the second mortgage have reduced the principal on the two loans $3,066. This leaves a balance on the first of $157,865 and on the second of $124,019, totaling $281,884. Deducting this from the approximate market value of $675,000 leaves an estimated equity of $393,116.)

Equity in Wildwood fourplex, market value $142,450
$220,000
(Principal payments reduce loan $1,130
for five months, leaving loan balance
of $77,550, resulting in equity of
$142,450.)

Money market balance	24,838
(Includes five months' interest of $994 at 10 percent annually.)	
Credit Union balance	4,509
(Includes $3,414 original balance plus $200 monthly for five months plus 6 percent interest for five months)	
Total net assets	$564,913

Twenty-one months after buying the Spruce Street house the net worth of the Wrights has progressed to $564,913. In less than two years they have accumulated over half a million and are considerably ahead of the four-year goal in Chapter 3 of $427,783.

CHAPTER 11

How Submetering
Saves Energy
and Makes Money

THERE WAS A time not long ago when utility companies paraded a constant stream of sales gimmicks to urge you to use more of their gas and electricity. If you hooked up an electric range they would give you a free toaster or other small energy-consuming appliance. If you put in a gas heater they would give you another energy-using freebie, perhaps a radio.

A FREE RANGE

Such token incentives were routinely offered by California's Pacific Gas and Electric Company. Sales appeals were intensified in areas where PG&E competed with another supplier of a different fuel, particularly in exhorting owners to switch energies.

In Sacramento, California, for example, PG&E was restricted to gas, and the Sacramento Municipal Utility District sold electricity on an exclusive basis. I was actually offered brand-new kitchen ranges for my new Sacramento apartments by PG&E, as a bonus for switching my order from electricity to gas, and by SMUD for switching from gas to electricity.

Electric companies like SMUD sponsored a national booster organization called Gold Medallion Homes, which paid bonuses to builders of all-electric homes.

An important continuing incentive to increase energy usage followed the old saw "The more you use the more you save," with a sliding scale downward in rate schedules. The more electricity and gas you used the lower your rate would be.

BE PATRIOTIC—SAVE ENERGY!

Utility companies have changed, as our energy resources have grown scarce, especially on rate schedules, from encouraging to discouraging energy usage. As a leading champion of energy savings, PG&E now begins with heavy penalties for high use. The more you use the more you pay, in order to discourage waste. Thus the median rate is about 50 percent more than the lowest Lifeline rate, and the spendthrift top rate is almost double the Lifeline base rate.

Advertising, monthly bulletins, and other promotional literature stress how PG&E is patriotically going all out to save energy. The company spent $30 million in 1983 in rebates for customer energy savings in commercial operations like my La Peralta Apartments. Increased energy usage requires more generators, which cost a lot more money than those already in service, and paying for them would require even more increases in rates. PG&E therefore utilizes every conceivable means in its own operations to save energy, and customers are encouraged to do the same.

POWER FROM MAGMA AND WIND

PG&E is a world leader in using electricity generated in the windswept sky and in the bowels of the earth, and we would all do well to follow its conservation lead on even the smallest scale. PG&E buys up to 618,000 kilowatts from thousands of generators turned by the wind sweeping from the Pacific Ocean over California's coastal hills.

Other PG&E operations serve as energy-saving inspirations to other utilities, and to single-family and multiple-unit homeowners. PG&E operates the world's largest geothermal energy plant, with a projected capacity of 1.5 million kilowatts, by harnessing scalding steam heated by superhot magma 5,000 feet below the surface.

The geothermal plant at the Geysers in Northern California takes advantage of a highly favorable operating depth, a lesson to us all to tailor our cost-cutting efforts to favorable conditions in our own environments. Most of the rest of the world has to go down four times as far as PG&E to reach the hot magma.

PG&E stresses that it is doing its part as a patriotic corporate body to save conventional oil and gas fuel by utilizing alternate sources, like wind and geothermal energy.

PERPETUAL POWER FROM FALLING WATER

PG&E is also the national investor-owned leader in hydroelectric power. The company explores every unused or underused possibility in the water-bountiful Sierras for additional power. Falling water is the cheapest conventional source of power if not so distant from points of use that it requires excessively long transmission lines.

Water may continue to produce electricity as it courses to a succession of downstream power plants. But, like spent fuel, it normally never returns to power the same generators, except as rain or snow carried back by clouds to the same watershed.

PG&E disproved the dictum that you can't reuse water power by engineering an ingenious never-ending use of Sierra hydroelectric power. In 1984 the company completed the Helms Pumped Storage Project on the Kings River, east of Fresno. Its three huge underground generators produce 1.2 million kilowatts, about half of PG&E's total hydro output. This is enough for one million customers, one-quarter of the total.

The perpetual-waterfall project works with two lakes, Court-right Reservoir above the power plant and Wishon Reservoir below. During peak hours, water flows at 4 million gallons a minute from the top lake through the spinning generators into the lower lake. In slack hours the swirling water is pumped by re-versed turbines from Wishon Reservoir back up to Courtright Lake, ready for another downhill cascade during the next peak hours.

MORE ENERGY CONSERVATION

Besides encouraging conventional solar usage PG&E explores more unorthodox solar potentials like direct voltaic battery power from the sun. In 1984 PG&E bought 37,000 kilowatts from seven experimental voltaic projects. Despite the antinuclear picketing and construction delays at earthquake-threatened Diablo Canyon, PG&E continues to save fossil fuels by exploring the long-range, fuel-efficient potential of nuclear power.

PG&E is looking at every possibility of cutting capacity re-quirements, spreading peak loads over longer periods and en-couraging customers to reduce or eliminate nonessential usage over peak periods.

Utility monitors keep thinking of ways to encourage customers to save energy. Excerpts from PG&E bulletins to customers ad-monish, "Leave your heating thermostat at 65 and your air con-ditioner at 75. If you don't have thermostat controls, install them. If you feel too cold in the winter, put on more clothes. If you feel too hot in the summer, take off more clothes! If you are chilled at night, don't turn on your electric blanket. Put on another blanket!"

Kathy Hyams, editor of the interesting and helpful monthly publication *PG&E Progress*, mailed to all four million customers, advises me, along with other pertinent information, "Our energy conservation programs save the equivalent of 2,754,800 barrels of oil annually."

WE DON'T IGNORE PG&E

As customers, Lucille and I usually discuss all of the PG&E suggestions. Some we don't take, some we follow, and some we modify. But we don't ignore them. Look at all the energy savings, reduced costs, and actual profits we made by following PG&E's suggestions about solar-heated hot water, which we installed at both our La Peralta Apartments and our home.

You can bet your life that we read with great interest a new letter from PG&E, asking permission to make a full energy-conservation survey of La Peralta. After the survey PG&E would make specific recommendations on ways to save more gas and electric energy. Based on usual results with our type of installations, the company predicted potential savings of about 50 percent in our present energy costs of about $40,000. Also, PG&E warned, energy rates were bound to rise significantly, which meant that future savings would be even greater. Here are the PG&E recommendations following the energy survey.

PG&E ENERGY UTILIZATION ANALYSIS,
Summary of Savings, La Peralta Apartments

KW Usage	KWH Savings	Therm Savings	Est. Cost	Payback Years	Annual Savings
1. 4	229,805		$49,000	2.6	$14,940
2. 2	12,940		$1,130	1	$1,160
3.	1,490		$70	½	$140
4.		2,800	-0-	Immediate	$1,570
5.		2,860	-0-	Immediate	$1,460
Totals 6	244,235	5,660	$50,200		$19,270

Recommendations

1. Master Meter Conversion
Install individual electric meters to replace the master in your 82 apart-

ments. When tenants become financially responsible they generally reduce their energy consumption at least 15%. You can lower your operating expense for the apartment usage by 100% where the tenants pay the energy bills. [Approved by owner.]

2. Lighting A
Install PL-9 fluorescent conversion kits to replace your 40-watt incandescent bulbs located in the 1st to 6th floor hallways, in the basement and stairways. This will increase your lighting levels and reduce your lamp replacement and maintenance costs. [Approved.]

3. Lighting B
Install a 4-lamp 34-watt fluorescent strip fixture to replace your 5-lamp 100-watt incandescent fixture located in the manager's office. This will maintain present lighting and last approximately 12 times longer than the incandescent bulbs. [Approved.]

4. Domestic hot water
Lower your domestic hot water temperature from 144 to 120 degrees. This will also improve the efficiency of your solar system. [Approved for 130 degrees.]

5. Space heating
Lower the thermostat on your central space heating boiler to 68 degrees. A 3% reduction in energy consumption is gained for every degree you lower the thermostat. [Approved.]

FIVE MONEY-SAVERS

I decided to follow all five PG&E recommendations, some on a modified basis. The analysis included "payback years," ranging from "Immediate" to a maximum of 2.6 years.

How did these recommendations tie in with my $2-for-$1 formula as a minimum value increase? Back to basics: A sound valuation of an income property is ten times the net annual income. (The increase in net and gross income is the same if you do not increase operating expenses.) For every $1 you increase net income or reduce operating costs annually you increase value $10. This means you break even in ten years for an item that annually gives you 10 percent of its cost in increased net income or in reduced expenses.

If the cost of the item is paid back in five years, it pays you 20 percent per year, and meets my $2-for-$1 minimum requirement. To translate the payback periods into values, the 2.6-year estimated payback for master meter conversion means approximately a $4-for-$1 value increase. A payback of 1.7 years means approximately a $6-for-$1 increase, a ten-month payback means approximately a $12-for-$1 increase.

Of course, all these costs are tax-deductible, either as repairs or as depreciation, cutting all the net costs and the payback periods in half in my 50 percent tax bracket.

DECISION TO CONVERT

Here was another decision—to proceed with the master meter conversion as soon as I received acceptable bids approximating the PG&E estimate of $49,000.

I decided to follow the three lighting recommendations as made. Our hot-water installation involved some heat loss because the central system, including the basement, covered seven stories. I had previously installed an adequate pump to keep the hot water circulating. This reduced heat loss and kept the temperature more uniform throughout the system.

After discussing the ideal delivery temperatures versus practical costs with various contractors and PG&E engineers, I decided to compromise with a hot-water thermostat setting of 130 degrees instead of the recommended 120. Our setting had been 130 when we installed our solar system, but tenants talked our maintenance man into pushing hot water to 144 degrees. I established 68 degrees as a fair temperature setting for central space heating.

PG&E gave a list of over a hundred properly licensed contractors covering Northern California, and mostly in the San Francisco Bay area. These were all acceptable as far as enabling La

Peralta to qualify for the PG&E subsidy given for a limited time to encourage immediate action. The subsidy was $50 for each meter installed for tenant rather than owner billing, and $1.75 per month to cover the cost of billing each submeter usage.

ENERGY SAVERS VS. SPENDTHRIFTS

PG&E estimated that having tenants pay for their individual usage would result in energy savings of 15 to 30 percent. Surveys had proved that most tenants favor individual meters, as they pay only for what they use and can save if they conserve. Any waste on a master meter has to be prorated by the owner among all tenants on an equal basis, with the conservationists paying the same as the spendthrifts.

Our PG&E engineer stated that most apartment buildings erected up to 1950 were equipped only with master meters, as this saved construction costs, and utility costs were then considered inconsequential. After 1950 the ongoing trend was to install individual tenant meters. Now that utility costs were skyrocketing, this trend was increasing.

There were two installation possibilities. One was to eliminate existing owner-paid master meters and install a utility company meter for each tenant, to be billed by PG&E. Second was to continue billing the owner on the master meter reading and installing submeters, one for each tenant. The owner could have his manager bill each tenant, or turn the task over to a bookkeeping firm specializing in this service, at the $1.75-per-meter fee subsidized by PG&E.

Submetering was by far the more popular practice, as it usually involved only minor rewiring. If the master meter was removed and each tenant was billed through a utility company meter, extensive rewiring would be required. Bringing all older wiring up to present city codes would be prohibitively expensive in most cases.

TENANT SUBMETERING

Five leading contractors bid on the submetering project. PG&E engineers and each contractor added to my education by pointing out various advantages of submetering rather than wiring each apartment to PG&E meters.

I had thought that a meter was a meter was a meter, and if you asked for bids on meters there wasn't much choice. I was advised that there were three major electric meter categories, called pin-and-jewel, electromechanical, and solid-state-electronic.

Most existing PG&E electric meters and all electric utility meters installed up to 1950 were pin-and-jewel-bearing mechanical meters. These were now considered obsolete, with inaccuracy beyond present tolerations. In 1950, General Electric produced an electromechanical meter, replacing gears and bearings with opposing magnets. Most electrical manufacturers concentrated on this type of meter after the GE patent ran out in 1960. This improved meter is now being replaced by yet more trouble-free solid-state electronic meters such as those manufactured by Fisher Pierce Meters.

Our contractors agreed with PG&E that even with submetering it would make no sense to install meters for our twenty-one sleeping rooms, which had no kitchens. Their common wiring would have to be replaced by complete new wiring from each of the units to new meters in the basement. Our seventy-three apartments, however, presented no major wiring problems, and submeters could be connected to them on a reasonable profit-making basis.

Five estimates for installing the seventy-three submeters with necessary wiring ranged from $150,000 to $41,370. The lowest bidder, McMillan Electric of San Francisco, and all its specifications were approved by PG&E. McMillan agreed to a 5 percent discount to $39,301 if I would give it the contract, which follows.

McMillan Electric

1515 So. Van Ness Ave. / San Francisco, CA 94110 / Phone 826-5110
Contractor's State License No. 268179-C10

GENERAL CONTRACT

THIS AGREEMENT, made this _____First_____ day of _____June_____ 19 _84_ , by and between

McMillan Electric Company , hereinafter called the Contractor, and

Name _Mr. Bill Nickerson_   _La Peralta Apts._

Address _184 13th Street,_ _____ City _____ _Oakland, California, 94612_

Address of Job _184 13th Street_ _____ City _____ _Oakland, California, 94612_
hereinafter called the Owner.

Witnesseth, That the Contractor and Owner for the considerations hereinafter named agree, as follows:

The Contractor agrees to furnish all material and labor and perform all work as described in the plans and specifications signed and accepted by the Owner.   Per quotation. (Delivered to you May 16th, 1984) for Fisher Pierce Meters, for the following apartments. Meters to be mounted in central location in the basement.

Apartment #201-#501 = 4	Apartment #108-#508 = 5
Apartment #102-#502 = 5	Apartment #109-#509 = 5
Apartment #103-#503 = 5	Apartment #110-#510 = 5
Apartment #104-#504 = 5	Apartment #111-#511 = 5
Apartment #205-#505 = 4	Apartment #112-#512 = 5
Apartment #206-#506 = 4	Apartment #116-#516 = 5
Apartment #107-#507 = 5	Apartment #117-#517 = 5
Apartment #251-#551 = 4	Apartment #600-xxxx = 1
	Apartment #601-xxxx = 1

This contract and installation subject to approval by Pacific Gas and Electric Master Meter Conversion Division.

A twelve month billing service (with option to terminate in six months) will be provided for each of the 73 apartments. The monthly bills will be bulk-mailed to the resident manager. The service will be provided by United Metering and Load Management Inc. for $1.75 per unit per month.

The undersigned owner agrees to pay the sum of $_39,301.00 representing 5% discount_
Payment to be made as follows:

Down payment. $8,000.00
Weekly   . . . . . $5,000.00   (for four weeks)
Balance   . . . .   Upon completion of job and approval by
                                          City Inspector, PGE and Dept. of Weights
                                          and Measures.

It is mutually agreed that this contract is assignable by the Contractor.
It is mutually agreed that the title in and to said improvements shall remain in the Contractor until the whole amount shall have been paid. It is mutually agreed that this instrument together with plans and specifications, if any, constitutes the agreement.
The Owner, or undersigned, represents that he is (they are) the title holder of record of the above mentioned premises upon which the work is to be done.
The Owner, or undersigned, acknowledges receipt of a true copy of this contract.
This contract shall not be binding on the contractor unless properly accepted by same. In the event of default in payment of any of said payments, or of any note, or of the sale of said land or building, the Contractor may declare the whole of said sum immediately due and payable plus court costs and reasonable Attorney's fees.
It is mutually agreed that this contract is not subject to cancellation except by the mutual consent of all parties thereto.
The Owner agrees that in the event of attempted cancellation by him of this contract after acceptance by the Contractor and before work is commenced, that he (the Owner) will reimburse the Contractor for all expenses incurred by the latter incidental to the contract, i.e., cost of time expended by the Contractor or his agents, cost of sending truck out to the Owner's premises, etc., in the form of liquidated damages as well as a reasonable attorney's fee.

Signed _Leo J. McMillan_ June 1, 1984   Signed _Wm Nickerson_ June 4, 1984
                                                                          Owner

_____Leo J. McMillan   Vice President_   Signed_____

GIVING TENANTS ENERGY CONTROL

The following letter was delivered to tenants in all seventy-three apartments that were to be connected to submeters.

M. Noah, Tenant
La Peralta Apartments   RE: Energy conservation/utilities

As an energy-and-cost-saving measure, the owner of the building will be converting the electric metering of this complex to individual meters. This will avoid having to raise rents merely to offset rising utility costs.

You will now have total control over your own energy use and over your energy costs. As a result, you will only be charged for the energy you use, not someone else's waste. In addition, the lowest baseline allowance from PG&E will be greater to individuals than is now received by the complex. This greater allowance per apartment should further reduce individual utility bills and control overall costs to the complex.

Fixer Upper Management will notify you as to when construction and conversion will begin. All workmen in the building will be representatives of PG&E or the contractor and will be fully bonded personnel.

When the actual changeover occurs, you will be without power for a maximum of three hours during the day. You will be given notification by signs posted in the building so that you may make any necessary arrangements.

You will enjoy the cost savings, the control of energy use, and, eventually, the savings in rent raises due to the savings to the complex through this energy conservation measure. We will make every effort to keep inconvenience to you during conversion to a minimum.

Sincerely,
Moira Pride, Property Manager
Fixer Upper Management Co.

Most of the tenants responded by stating that they were happy to be able to control their own electricity and to pay only for the electricity they used.

$5,232 NET COST FOR $39,301 JOB!

On a no-deduction-or-credit basis, for an owner who pays no income taxes and gets no utility rebate, the submetering project pays back within three years, earning a profit of 3.4 to 1.

A review of our costs and credits at La Peralta reveals the following:

Total cost	$39,301
Depreciation, federal and California, five-year period, 20% per year	−22,559
(Federal applies to balance after deducting half of $3,930 federal energy credit, $39,301 less $1,965, or $37,336; 50% maximum tax bracket equals 50% savings of $18,668. California applies to balance after deducting full state energy credit, $39,301 less $3,930, or $35,371; 11% maximum tax bracket equals 11% savings of $3,891.)	
PG&E rebate, 73 apartments at $50 each	−3,650
Energy tax credits: 10% federal, $3,930; 10% California, $3,930	−7,860
Net cost	$5,232

At this net cost the submetering project actually pays for itself in five months, figuring annual savings of $13,446. This is the amount that PG&E estimates for the seventy-three submetered apartments, allocating 90 percent of all energy usage to these larger rental units. The increased value of $134,460 is 25.7 times our net cost, making a $25.7-to-$1 return.

As with other projects I have mentioned, when a real estate investor semiretires and starts paying income taxes, he can at least take advantage of more tax credits! Incidentally, credits are not automatically given to you. You have to ask for them by listing them on your tax return.

GIVE CREDIT WHERE CREDIT IS DUE

There is a story I heard about a misanthropic slum landlord commonly called Mr. Scrooge by his unhappy tenants because he wouldn't spend a penny for painting or repairs. It reminds us you usually get what's coming to you.

Scrooge died, and he arrived at the Pearly Gates and asked to be admitted.

St. Peter appeared and asked, "What have you done to help your fellow man?"

"One Christmas I passed a Salvation Army girl ringing her bell," the landlord replied, "and I put a dollar in her pot."

"Is that all?" St. Peter asked.

"No," the slum landlord said. "One Easter Sunday I passed a church and heard the beautiful organ music. I went inside and put a dollar in the collection plate. Don't I get credit for my two dollars?"

With this, St. Peter turned to his secretary for corroboration. "Do we have a record of that?" he asked.

"Yes," the secretary said. "Will that be all?"

"No," St. Peter told his secretary. "Give him his two dollars back and tell him to go to hell!"

CHAPTER 12

Should You Scrap Your Old Gray Boiler?

MY PG&E REPRESENTATIVE also recommended that I consider converting the gas-fired central steam space-heating system to individual tenant-metered wall-mounted gas heaters. Costs were uncertain, depending on the capacity of our present gas and electric lines and the necessity for venting.

The electric installation might require running new power lines from PG&E and through the building. Gas heaters would require vents and additional gas pipes. I promised to investigate costs for both gas and electric individual heaters.

GAS VS. ELECTRICITY

The PG&E rep said her company favored converting central gas heat to individual gas heat, which would save gas. It also favored converting electric heaters to gas, which would save electricity. But it frowned on converting gas heat to electric, because in the long run, for the same results electric power consumes more energy. For example, PG&E never converts electricity directly into gas, but much of its electric power is generated by using gas-fired boilers.

I said that I would consider gas as my number-one choice for individual heaters if costs were feasible. I felt free to use individual electric heaters if they bottom-lined as more cost-effective and gas-heater installation proved highly cost-prohibitive. Perhaps neither gas nor electric individual heaters would appear profitable. In this case I would welcome any suggestions to make the present heating systems more productive at less energy cost.

BATTLE OVER THE HEAT THERMOSTAT

La Peralta would start conserving energy as mentioned by immediately reducing the heat thermostat in the resident manager's office from 72 to 68 degrees, following PG&E's suggestion. This was still higher than in several nearby federal, state, and county buildings, where the heat thermostats were set at 65. So our tenants shouldn't grumble too much at a heat level of 68. They shouldn't, but there are always some tenants who complain no matter where the thermostat is set.

As a matter of fact, after receiving previous PG&E literature urging everybody to save energy, I had several months before I ordered the heat thermostat lowered from 72 to 68. Then the resident manager received complaints from querulous little old ladies wearing diaphanous dressing gowns when they came to the lobby on colder days for mail, and from distraught young mothers demanding hothouse temperatures in which to bathe their babies.

Influenced, no doubt, by a couple of $5 tips, our former maintenance man was persuaded to push the thermostat control up to its pre-scarce-energy level of 72. Threats by PG&E to charge penalty rates unless we conserved energy, and the company's written recommendations, helped convince our resident manager and new maintenance man that the heat thermostat should stay at a firm 68. I ordered that the setting was not to be changed without my specific approval.

While the young mothers and elderly tenants complained that there was not enough heat, some healthy young adults griped to the resident manager that it was too hot. Typical of messages slipped under the office door was this note: "Why do you turn our apartment into an oven when we are enjoying such lovely weather? We have to open all our windows and waste all that heat to keep from roasting to death!"

In heating, as in other matters, I've learned never to expect a consensus among my many tenants. For perfectly legitimate reasons, each tenant may prefer a different temperature. With a central heating system controlled by one thermostat it is impossible to satisfy the demands of all tenants. Tenants are happier and resident managers and maintenance people enjoy a more peaceful life with less tenant bickering if each resident controls his own heat.

If the little old lady and the young mother want hothouse heat, and are willing to pay for it, why shouldn't they have it? It isn't feasible to turn the whole building into a sauna. In income properties ranging from two units to thousands, most rental owners and tenants agree that individually controlled separate heaters are the answer. If comparison of installation costs and energy savings was anywhere near encouraging, I was anxious to scrap our old gray boiler and install individual heaters for each tenant.

FOUR BASIC ALTERNATIVES

There were four basic alternatives to choose from.

1. Rejuvenate the present boiler, steam pipes, valves, and radiators.
2. Install individual gas heaters in all rental units.
3. Install individual electric heaters in all rental units.
4. Install a combination of electric and gas heaters, with either one or the other in each rental unit.

In order to make an intelligent decision that would produce the most profit at the least cost in money and energy, it was necessary to obtain estimates on all four alternatives.

SHOULD WE REJUVENATE THE PRESENT BOILER SYSTEM?

The steam heating system had been installed in 1908. Oil-fueled burners turned water into low-pressure steam, which was forced into radiators in the rental units. In the early 1930s the oil burners were converted to consume natural gas. Otherwise the entire system had seen little change since 1908.

The old gray boiler was soundly built and still rendered fairly efficient service. PG&E experts expected it to be about 50 percent fuel-efficient, about average for this type of installation. But our boiler system was doing better than average at 65 percent fuel efficiency.

Three different heating contractors stated that we were lucky. Only superior maintenance had held the old boiler together, and it had survived many years past its burial time. We investigated the possibility of scrapping the old boiler and replacing it with a new boiler that was designed to save between 25 percent and 30 percent in energy costs. Bids ran from $95,000 to $49,000. The lowest bid was from a reputable heating contractor and included the details on the following proposal:

Install a new Bryan Steam Boiler M#CL90. The installation will also include the following:

1. New return piping in the basement to the new boiler
2. New automatic water feed system
3. 3 Auto Air vents in the basement
4. Electrical hookups to new boiler (low and high voltage)
5. New steam header piping in basement to boiler.
6. New flue pipe to boiler
7. Blow-down manifold
8. Chemical-treatment piping for boiler water
9. Replacement of all radiator valves on existing radiators
10. Repair of return lines to existing radiators
11. Testing of all radiators
12. Removal of old boiler and materials

13. All material and labor for the above specifications for the sum of $49,000. ⅓ down upon contract acceptance. Balance on completion.

The $49,000 cost could be 100 percent depreciated in ten years. In my top tax bracket the eventual depreciation deductions would save 50 percent on federal income taxes and 11 percent on California income taxes. This came to $24,500 and $5,390, totaling $29,890, making my net cost after depreciation $19,110.

At a 25 percent annual savings of $3,000 on approximately $12,000 in total heating fuel costs, the new boiler would pay for itself in 6.4 years. This gave a capital return of close to 16 percent. A new boiler system would also save some of the nominal repair bills. Although boiler system repair bills averaged less than $1,000 a year, this figure would no doubt increase with each year of added use.

Basically, in my tax brackets, the new boiler would save enough repair and energy costs to warrant consideration. If installed, the owner would still pay all heating costs, and individual tenants would still have no control over the amount of heat they received. A final determination would depend on results from checking other alternatives.

SHOULD WE INSTALL INDIVIDUAL GAS HEATERS IN ALL HOUSING UNITS?

Four bids from PG&E-recommended contractors for installing individual gas heaters in all housing units ran from $450,000 to $262,000. Following are details of the lowest estimate:

Install 118 gas heaters, including the following:
1. Install 1 heater in each sleeping room.
2. Install 1 heater in each studio apartment.
3. Install 1 heater in each 1-bedroom apartment.
4. Install 2 heaters in each 2-bedroom apartment.
5. Install 3 heaters in each 3-bedroom apartment.
6. Install complete new gas piping to each heater, including

apartments which now have gas ranges. Existing pipes too small for both ranges and heaters.

7. This contract acceptable upon acceptance by the City of Oakland and their approval of all necessary permits and inspections.

8. All above labor and material furnished for the sum of $262,000. 10% down payment at start. Weekly progress payments.

I checked with City Hall as to the number of individual gas or electric heaters required by code. The heating inspector said, "One for each living room and one for each bedroom. That's the same as the number of radiators on your boiler system. Of course, each heater has to have adequate capacity."

City Hall requirements totaled 170 individual heaters distributed as follows:

	Heaters per Rental Unit	Total Heaters
21 sleeping rooms	1	21
23 studio apartments	1	23
30 1-bedroom apartments	2	60
14 2-bedroom apartments	3	42
6 3-bedroom apartments	4	24
	Total	170

The low bidder's 118 heaters were fifty-two short of City Hall requirements, and he had not stated the BTU ratings. His bid of $262,000 represented $2,220 per heater. Multiplying by the 170 needed heating units brought the comparable cost to $377,400. This was $115,440 more than the original bid, a warning example of the need to double-check the adequacy of low bids.

I contacted the low bidder and advised him that the city required 170 heaters with adequate specified BTU ratings. What would his bid be for the revised total?

He said City Hall was always asking more than necessary, but he would have to meet their demands. "I'll check their BTU specs and call you back."

He phoned later and said, "My bid for 170 heaters should be

$400,000. But I'll do you a special favor and give you a price of $375,000."

A DISCOURAGING BOTTOM LINE

At the lowest corrected bid of $375,000, my tax savings after 100 percent depreciation in ten years would be $187,500 at the 50 percent federal level and $41,250 at the 11 percent state level. The total of $228,750 would make my net cost after depreciation $146,250.

The twenty-one sleeping rooms, for which the owner customarily pays utilities, would have individual heaters and thermostats, but would still be connected to the owner's master meters. Their heating space represented under 10 percent of the total.

Heaters in each of the seventy-three apartments would run to individual gas meters. The apartment bills for heating would be transferred from the owner to the tenants in lieu of an annual or semiannual rent raise. This meant that the owner would save about 90 percent of the $12,284 annual cost for space heating, an estimated savings of $11,056.

At a saving of $11,056 in annual energy costs, it would take about 13.2 years for the individual gas heaters to pay for themselves, an annual return of 7.6 percent. This low return was well below $1 for $1, let alone meeting our minimum goal of $2 for $1. It appeared too high a price to pay for adding to tenant happiness with individually controlled heat.

SHOULD WE INSTALL INDIVIDUAL ELECTRIC HEATERS IN ALL RENTAL UNITS?

I was anxious to compare potential costs of converting to individual electric heaters. I had thought that there was only one basic kind of electric baseboard heater. Just as I previously learned that there was more than one kind of meter, I found that there were major differences in heaters. Where older heaters were dry, most new electric baseboard heaters contained freeze-protected water, producing a radiant heat that saved energy.

City hall had already advised that a total of 170 heaters were required for either gas or electric energy. Before obtaining bids I checked with City Hall as to required electric heater capacity and with PG&E engineers as to desirable capacities. For the twenty-one sleeping rooms the required capacity was 750 watts for normally cold weather, and 1,000 watts was desirable for colder-than-normal weather. For all seventy-three apartment living rooms, the capacity was 1,500 watts required, 2,000 watts desirable. For the seventy-six apartment bedrooms, capacity was 1,000 watts required, 1,500 desirable.

After reviewing desirable and ideal capacities with PG&E, I decided to consider 2,000-watt, 6,826-BTU-per-hour heaters in all seventy-three living rooms, and 1,500-watt, 5,120-BTU heaters in all ninety-seven sleeping rooms and apartment bedrooms.

Four contractors submitted bids to install 170 baseboard-mounted electric thermal heaters, together with necessary wiring and panels to carry additional power.

Bids ran from $300,000 to $133,600, showing wild fluctuations with similar specifications. The lowest acceptable bid was made by McMillan Electric, the same firm which was working on the submetering contract. There was a marked difference in the methods of the highest and lowest bidders. I learned that the $300,000 bidder arrived at a horseback estimate of $150,000, based on previous experience. He then doubled his estimate in order to pay for unseen contingencies and leave a high profit. McMillan's vice president, Leo McMillan, meticulously reviewed costs of labor and material and possible contingencies, then submitted the lowest sound bid on which his firm could expect to make a reasonable profit. Details of McMillan's successful bid follow.

1. Furnish and install all required labor and materials to provide 170 Intertherm Softheat Permanent Baseboard Heaters. Each living room to have a 2,000-watt heater. Each bedroom and

sleeping room to have a 1,500-watt
heater. Each heater to carry a 10-year
warranty.

Cost of heaters	$40,000.00

2. Furnish and install a new 1,200-am-
pere 120/208 volt, three-phase, four-
wire main electric switchboard, to
accommodate existing and new electrical loads, and to replace existing
800-amp main switchboard.

Cost of main switchboard	30,000.00

3. Furnish and install new electric
panels and feeders distribution system.

Cost of panels and feeders	20,000.00

4. Complete wiring as required to install new wiring and replace old wiring, from 6 floors to basement.

Cost of wiring	43,600.00
Total contract amount	$133,600.00

All our work will be done in a neat and workmanlike manner
and will meet the requirements of both the Oakland Inspection Department and local PG&E's requirements.

Progress invoicing based on percentage of completed work.

Leo J. McMillan, Vice President
McMillan Electric Company

THE ONLY WAY TO GO

Double-checking our previously mentioned four alternatives, the
$133,600 cost of installing 170 electric heaters obviously was
more attractive than the $375,000 cost of 170 gas heaters. The
$786-per-unit cost for the electric heaters also ruled out combining
them with gas heaters at their unit cost of $2,206.

I had expected a considerable discount on installing gas heaters
in the forty-four apartments where we had gas kitchen ranges and

could merely extend existing gas pipes. It developed that existing gas lines were not large enough to handle the additional load of gas heaters. New piping would have to be run to all ninety-four units, canceling any discount that might make some gas heaters competitive.

Electric heaters in the seventy-three apartments would be connected to submeters. As with gas metering, the seventy-three submetered apartments would save about 90 percent of heating costs to the owner, amounting to $11,056 per year. Heaters in the twenty-one sleeping rooms, which did not warrant submetering, would have individual thermostats, but would still be connected to the owner's master electric meters.

The 100 percent depreciation over ten years of the $133,600 electric heater cost would amount to net savings of 50 percent of $66,800 for federal income tax deductions and 11 percent or $14,696 for California deductions, totaling $81,496. Deducting this from the installation price of $133,600 left a net cost of $52,104. This would be paid for by the $11,056 annual energy savings in 4.7 years, giving an annual return of 21 percent. The return on net investment was $2.1 for $1, in addition to other offsetting costs and the advantage of enabling tenants to regulate their own heat.

Replacing the seventy-six-year-old boiler at a basic cost of $49,000 looked like a step backward in long-range heating plans, especially with continually rising energy costs. As utility rates escalated the owner's bills for boiler gas would rise, whereas for individual heaters the owner's savings would keep increasing. Also tenants would save in the long run by having individual controls, especially those who were conservation-minded.

An overall comparison of actual costs should take into account the needed replacement of the boiler if individual heaters were not installed. Deducting the net cost after taxes of $19,110 for retaining a boiler system from the $52,104 net cost of 170 electric heaters leaves a balance of $32,994 as the true difference to account for. This pays back from the $11,056 energy savings in just under three years, representing a 33 percent annual return and an increased value of $3 for $1.

THE OLD GRAY MARE

The old gray boiler, like the old gray mare, had performed remarkably well, but she wasn't what she used to be. With changing times and rising fuel costs, the Peralta heating system had seen its best days, and we decided it needed to be scrapped after all.

The tenants, all of them, were thrilled to learn they would soon enjoy individual heat control. "I just love to control my own heat," commented one attractive widow, thanking me for initiating the change. "I haven't felt really hot since my dear husband died!"

CHAPTER 13

The Silverado Trail
to $1 Million in 3 Years

CHAPTER 10 LEFT the Wrights on December 10, 1982, with a net worth of $564,913. They decided to coast through the holidays and start looking in earnest in January for a larger property with from twenty-four to a hundred units.

In the meantime they assessed the general possibilities open to them for buying, selling, or trading. Since they had disposed of the Spruce Street house and $5,000 second mortgage, they had two investment properties remaining and $29,347 in cash to move on the investment board like players in a game of chess.

DETERMINING SOME MAJOR POSSIBLE MOVES

1. All of their $564,913 investment assets could be committed to a sizable purchase in the $2 to $5 million range.
2. Their two property equities of $535,566 could be committed to a similar property in the $2 to $5 million range, with all cash held in reserve and all or part spent for improvements.
3. The Paradise Apartments equity of $393,116 could be traded by itself for a purchase in the $1 to $5 million range.
4. The Wildwood fourplex equity of $142,450 could be traded

by itself for a purchase in the $250,000 to $1 million range.

5. All or part of the $24,838 money market balance and/or the $4,509 credit union savings could be used to sweeten any of the above equity trades for larger properties or as all or part of a new cash-down purchase.

6. A newly created subsidiary mortgage or mortgages could be traded as a down payment, secured by all or part of each property equity or both property equities. This option offers myriad variations.

LOOKING FOR BIGGER FIXER-UPPER APARTMENTS

Over New Year's weekend the Wrights looked over for-sale ads in the *Metropole News*. On January 3, 1983, a Monday, they started calling interesting prospects indicated in the ads.

They also phoned realtors with whom they had previous contacts or dealings, including Patti Arthur, who had sold them the Spruce Street house, and Cindy Seekum, who had sold them the Wildwood fourplex. They told the realtors that they were again looking for fixer-upper Nickerson Deal apartments and would like to see any properties with from twenty-four to a hundred units that offered good possibilities for improvements.

Patti Arthur said that she specialized in single-family homes, but she would check with others in her office who handled apartments. Cindy Seekum and other realtors specializing in apartment sales asked the Wrights to give them exclusive sales listings on both the Wildwood fourplex and Paradise Apartments.

The Wrights replied that they first wanted to find a good buy before they made any commitment on their present properties. Over the next six weeks they looked at various properties and found some that looked interesting but were impossibly high-priced for their poor condition and for their present income. Some that had potential were ruled out because of unworkable financing, adamant refusals to negotiate, or other drawbacks.

On the Saturday morning of Lincoln's birthday, February 12, the Wrights spotted the following ad in the *Metropole News*.

SILVERADO APTS. SALE!
30-unit bargain!
Priced to sell—$395,000!
Don't Delay! Phone Today!

Tomorrow may be too late!
PHONE FRANCIS MEEKER
Meeker & Mitchman
Realtors 869-4404

The Wrights had two other properties to inspect, but decided to
postpone checking them for the present and concentrate on the
Silverado. Karen phoned Francis Meeker and made an appointment for one-thirty that afternoon in his office.

Meeker had a small two-desk office near the Silverado Apartments. He was a tall, thin, effeminate, and nervous chain smoker.
"This is a real bargain that I just got the listing on. I'll take you
out to see it as soon as my partner gets back. There's only the
two of us, and we like to have somebody here on a busy weekend
like this. You can look over this statement while we're waiting.
Don't hesitate to ask if you have any questions." The realtor
handed the Wrights a copy each of the following statement.

Silverado Apartments, Statement of Income and Expense
5907 Silverado Trail, Metropole, Columbia

PRICED TO SELL! $395,000!

Present financing: $220,000 8% Interest (Orig. $260,000, 30 years)
Payable $1,908 monthly, including interest
TERMS: Cash down to loan $175,000
Improvements: Two-story frame & stucco main building, with twenty
garages in rear. Spanish modern architecture in level garden setting.
Thirty apartments. Ten 3-room apts. & twenty 2-room apts. All
include stoves and refrigerators. Excellent rental location with city
bus stop in front of building and convenient shopping. Reasonably
priced rents for area. Needs minor repairs. Consistent 100% occupancy with no vacancies!
Lot size: Approx. 80′ frontage × 300′.

GROSS ANNUAL INCOME   **$56,832.00**
Rent schedule January 15, 1983

Apt.#	Rms.	Rent per Month	Apt.#	Rms.	Rent per Month	Apt.#	Rms.	Rent per Month
101	2	$140	102	2	$140	103	3	$ 180
104	3	180	105	2	140	106	2	140
107	2	140	108	2	140	109	2	140
110	2	140	111	3	180	112	3	180
113	2	140	114	2	140	115	3 Mgr.	180
201	2	140	202	2	140	203	3	180
204	3	180	205	2	140	206	2	140
207	2	140	208	2	140	209	2	140
210	2	140	211	3	180	212	3	180
213	2	140	214	2	140	215	3	180
					20 garages @ 5.00			100
					Coin laundry net 25% of gross			36

	Total monthly income	$4,736

ANNUAL EXPENSES   **$18,289.22**

Advertising	$ 286.00
City license	255.60
*Manager & janitor (#115 at $180 plus $90 month)	3,240.00
Maintenance & repairs not handled by manager & janitor	1,142.00
Insurance	631.86
Taxes	4,329.34
Electricity & gas	4,391.14
Garbage collection	324.00
Manager telephone	136.72
Water & sewer service	890.56
Supplies & miscellaneous	970.00
Vacancy allowance 3% of rent schedule	1,692.00

	Total annual expenses	$18,289.22

Net Annual Income	$38,542.78

*Manager & janitor handle all minor maintenance and repairs.

Inspection: Contact Resident Manager, Mrs. Gladys Bolger, Apt 115. Phone 569-2436.

Note: The above figures are provided by owner. While Meeker & Mitchman Realtors have reasonable belief that statement is true, they are not responsible for its accuracy.

MEEKER & MITCHMAN REALTORS
6240 Silverado Trail
Metropole, Columbia
Phone 869-4404
See Francis Meeker

WHY ISN'T THE BROKER RESPONSIBLE FOR HIS FIGURES?

After looking over the Silverado statement and making a few notes, Karen Wright asked, "Why aren't you responsible for your figures? Haven't you checked them so you know they are accurate?"

"That's the usual escape clause most brokers use," the broker replied. "We've checked most of the figures the owner gave us, but we can't guarantee them. It pays for you to check everything that you feel you need to."

Norman Wright asked, "What do you mean, 'Needs minor repairs'?"

"Oh, there's a little painting and a little plumbing and a little electric work that needs to be taken care of. It doesn't amount to all that much. You'll have to see for yourself."

"Instead of just a little, it sounds like quite a bit of everything needs repairs," said Norman.

"Why is the owner selling if they have 'consistent 100% occupancy'?" asked Karen.

"Well, I hate to tell you this, but you need to find out sooner or later. The place keeps running full, like it is now, but there are six tenants out of thirty that aren't paying any rent. So the Benders, that's the owners, aren't collecting the income they should. That's one reason they're selling. Another is, they don't keep the place up. They spend every cent they do collect and don't pay their bills. The tax collector is about ready to foreclose because they owe five years' back taxes, close to $25,000 with interest. Their credit is shot and they're desperate to raise some money."

At this point, Meeker's partner, Butch Mitchman, a burly man in cowboy hat and boots, walked in through the rear door from the parking lot. After introductions Meeker continued.

"I don't know what got into me. I guess after me blabbing all this stuff about the owners' problems, you don't want to waste time looking at the property."

"Looks like you certainly have a lot of management problems," said Norman. "But we might as well go ahead and look the apartments over."

"We appreciate your being honest with us," said Karen. "That's always the best policy. If the place doesn't look too bad, maybe we can figure out some way to fix it up and take the problems off the owners' hands."

THE SCRUFFIEST YARD IN THE NEIGHBORHOOD

The Silverado had the most unkempt-looking yard in a block of fairly desirable-looking homes and apartments. All the rest had attractive green lawns and shrubbery. The Silverado shrubbery against the building, across the front, and down both sides was overgrown and turning brown for lack of water. The lawn between the sidewalk and shrubbery, across the front, and halfway down one side to the entrance had some bare spots. The grass had a yellowish tinge, thirsting for water, and was badly in need of mowing.

The heavy wire glass at the top of the main front door was cracked. A red brick was wedged between the door and the frame on the handle side.

"Their intercom and lock system isn't working, so the tenants can't unlock the door to admit guests," explained Meeker. "That's why they have that brick to keep the door from locking, so guests can come right in."

Meeker escorted the Wrights to apartment 115. At the top of the door a brass sign read "Manager." At his knock a feminine voice inside asked, "Who is it?"

"This is Mr. Meeker from the real estate office. The Benders sent me to see you."

A woman weighing about 300 pounds opened the door. She was wearing paint-stained white overalls. Meeker introduced the Wrights as prospective buyers and introduced the manager as Mrs. Bolger. He told her, "If you are cooperative and answer all the Wrights' questions, they might want to keep you on as manager if they happen to buy the building."

"We'd like to go over this statement with you," said Karen. "Has anything changed since the Benders gave this information to Mr. Meeker? Are all the apartments actually rented at the prices shown on this sheet? It seems odd that all the twos are $140 and all the threes are $180."

"So far as I know that information is all correct. Those rents as listed are the rents every tenant is supposed to pay. But two of the three-room apartments and four of the two-room apartments haven't paid any rent for several months."

"If they don't pay rent, why don't you evict them?" asked Norman. "It usually shouldn't take more than a month or so to get rid of an out-and-out deadbeat."

"That's all it used to take when we had a lawyer from the Apartment Association. Then Mrs. Bender figured she would save the lawyer's fees by going to court and handling the evictions herself. She tried it through the Small Claims Court instead of the regular court that the lawyer used. She got judgments from Small Claims, but then the trouble began. The tenants got Legal Aid to appeal for them, claiming that the apartments were uninhabitable. The judge ordered an inspection by City Hall. When the inspector got here the tenants had damaged wiring and plumbing and plaster walls and ceilings. And they dumped garbage all over the place. All six evictions are still tied up by Legal Aid. The six deadbeats even tried to organize a rent strike by all the tenants, but none of the others would have a thing to do with it."

The Wrights looked at each other knowingly. If they bought

the Silverado there was no question that they would immediately turn the deadbeat problem over to their Apartment Association's attorney, who specialized in swift and sure evictions.

INSPECTION REVEALS FIXER-UPPER NEEDS

The main two-story building housed thirty apartments. In the rear of the lot was a single-story twenty-car garage. Inspection of the buildings revealed a need for complete indoor and outdoor painting and yard cleanup. There was leaky plumbing and loose wiring, especially in the six nonpaying apartments. Drab gray carpets were somewhat threadbare in the halls and most of the apartments.

All of the apartments were fairly spacious. All ten of the three-room apartments had a fairly large living room, bedroom, bathroom, and kitchen, with a dining area at the end of the kitchen. Eight of the three-room apartments had a floor space of 800 square feet. The manager's apartment, number 115, and 215, above it, each had a small office at the entrance and a total of 960 square feet.

Each of the twenty two-room apartments had 600 square feet, including a fairly large living room, bathroom, and kitchen, with a dining area at the end of the kitchen. At the end of each living room was a large closet holding a folding double bed behind the wall. There was also a built-in chest at one end of the closet and a rod holding clothes hangers at the other end.

Norman asked Mrs. Bolger, "Aren't you and your husband supposed to mow the lawn and keep up the yard?"

"Yes, we are. But we're supposed to get $90 cash for yardwork plus minor maintenance like cleaning out stopped-up sinks and toilets. The Benders stopped paying us any cash when the six tenants stopped paying them. We told them we wouldn't do the work till we got paid for it. We get our free apartment for showing and renting apartments. And we're supposed to be paid $5 extra an hour for painting. The Benders stopped paying us for that, too, so my husband and I stopped painting."

The Wrights told Meeker and Mrs. Bolger that they would have to bring their contractor to look over the buildings before they could decide whether the project had possibilities.

MONEY-MAKER OPPORTUNITIES

Driving back to their home, the Wrights discussed the potential of the Silverado. "We've looked at similar buildings in that area that got at least twice as much rent," said Karen. "All we have to do is paint and fix it up and we should make a big profit by doubling the rents."

"Yeah, the fixed-up studios should go to $280 and the one-bedrooms to $360," said Norman. "Also, we should make quite a bit more income by collecting all the rents. Our attorney will make short work of evicting those deadbeats."

"There was one little extra money-maker opportunity I noticed," said Karen. "Did you spot it?"

"No, I didn't notice anything but painting and general cleanup and repairs, such as we've done before."

"Those twenty studio apartments are all big enough to convert to one-bedrooms," said Karen. "That kind of a change could make quite an extra bonus, because they ought to be worth $360 after we convert them. All we need to do is convert the kitchen to a bedroom, take out the wall bed and replace it with a convertible sofa, and put a compact kitchen in the wall-bed space."

"Say, that is a good possibility! I'm anxious to have Jack Armstrong check out the cost for that job and everything else."

Karen said, "Let's have him give us an estimate as soon as possible."

Armstrong and the Wrights were able to make an appointment with Mrs. Bolger Sunday afternoon. Armstrong made copious notes and sketches and said he could give a firm estimate by the next evening, subject to verifying some material costs and sub-bids. The following evening Armstrong met with the Wrights.

Armstrong said, "I've helped several investors like you become rich and I've been wanting to buy fixer-uppers myself. But my wife won't let me. Amy is too scared that we might go broke."

"With your experience you should do exceptionally well," said Karen. "I don't think Amy has a thing to worry about."

"We appreciate your helping us get ahead and hope you can talk your wife into becoming an owner," said Norman.

"Thank you both," said Armstrong. "It's a pleasure to work with you, and I'm glad to give you the best deal I can. I'll just have to keep working on my wife." He presented the following estimate.

ESTIMATE OF PROPOSED WORK

Silverado Apartments,
5907 Silverado Trail, Metropole, Columbia

Project 1:

Carpet all halls and all apartment living rooms and bedrooms	$14,500
Install new linoleum 30 kitchens and dining areas	6,150
Install new indoor-outdoor carpet 30 bathrooms	3,900
Complete painting over new and old work, all inside halls and apartments and all exterior, including main building and garages, and including finished patching of all holes	12,500
Trim shrubbery and reseed lawns	600
Overall repairs, including electrical, plumbing and audio-electronic system between entrance and individual apartments	5,500
SUBTOTAL	43,150
10% contractor overhead	4,315
10% contractor profit	4,315
Total	51,780

Project 2:
Convert 20 studio apartments to 20 1-bedroom apartments

Clean out existing kitchen cabinets, etc. and install new bedroom closets	
Install compact kitchens in place of large wall-bed closets	34,000
10% contractor overhead	3,400
10% contractor profit	3,400
(Net additional if combined with Project 1)	
Total	40,800
Grand total both projects	92,580

The Wrights checked the feasibility of Projects 1 and 2, separately and combined. They developed the following income and expense estimates.

NEW INCOME AND EXPENSE SCHEDULE ON COMPLETION OF PROJECT 1

	NEW TOTALS
10 3-room apartments increased from $180 to $360 each	$3,600.00
20 2-room apartments increased from $140 to $280 each	5,600.00
20 garages increased from $5 to $10 each	200.00
Coin laundry increased from 25% to 50% of gross income	72.00
TOTAL MONTHLY INCOME	$9,472.00
TOTAL ANNUAL INCOME	$113,664.00
Annual expenses ($18,289.22 plus $180 monthly and $2,160 annual increase for manager's free apartment)	20,449.22
New annual net income	93,214.78
Present scheduled net income with all rents collected	38,542.78

Increased annual net income after repairs
and improvements   54,672.00

Increased capital valuation $546,720, as-
suming that the property can be bought for
approximately $385,000

The increase in value for an estimated expenditure of $51,780 represents a gratifying profit of 1,055.85 percent, over ten times the improvement cost. If advantageous purchase and financial arrangements can be made, the Silverado looks like another high profit maker if only Project 1 is undertaken. Project 2 is bound to pay a fair profit if combined with Project 1, but it pays to examine it as a separate potential.

NEW INCOME AND EXPENSE SCHEDULE ON COMPLETION OF PROJECT 2

Project 2 is converting twenty two-room apartments to twenty three-room apartments—from efficiency studios to one-bedroom apartments. The rent for studios is estimated to increase to $280 under Project 1. The additional increase from Project 2 would be $80 per unit, the difference between $280 and $360, the expected increase in monthly rents for one-bedroom apartments. Twenty apartments times $80 each makes $1,600 monthly, an annual increase of $19,200.

Since there would be no increase in expenses, this net increases the capital value by $192,000. The increase in value from the $40,800 estimated expenditure for Project 2 would be 470.58 percent. A profit of 4.7 times cost would certainly be worthwhile for the Project 2 conversion alone.

TACKLING BOTH PROJECTS

After the Wrights decided to tackle both projects, pending satisfactory purchase and financing agreements, they calculated the figures for the combined work. The net annual increases in income of $54,672 plus $19,200 would total $73,872. As a reward for total repair and improvement expenditures of $92,580, the increased capital value would be $738,720, making a profit of 797.9 percent or close to eight times the fixer-upper costs.

Rejected bids from two reputable contractors came to $149,000 and $195,000.

WHAT ARE NEGOTIATION POTENTIALS?

The Wrights were convinced that the Silverado had an extremely good profit potential and was not likely to be on the market for long. Some buyers seeking perfection would pass it by, but others willing to improve fixer-uppers were bound to recognize the potential and might equal or surpass the Wrights' plans. As occasionally happens, the asking price, in view of the improvement potential, already appeared to represent a bargain.

The Wrights decided to avoid delays and to raise their negotiation sights closer than usual to the $395,000 asking price. They gave Francis Meeker an opening offer on February 16, 1983, to exchange their Wildwood fourplex, "subject to the loan balance of $77,550," for the Silverado Apartments, "subject to the existng $220,000 loan." The offer was also "subject to obtaining financing satisfactory to buyers to pay for repairs and improvements of the Silverado Apartments." Adding the Wrights' Wildwood equity of $142,450 to the $220,000 Silverado loan which the Wrights would be taking over represented an opening exchange offer of $362,450 for the Silverado.

THE SELLERS ARE DESPERATE FOR CASH

Meeker said, "There's no use talking to the Benders about a trade where no cash could be raised. They are desperate for cash to pay off their pressing debts, including $25,000 in back taxes on the Silverado. Also, even if you offer a cash down payment, the

Benders would not want to wait very long for you to arrange the financing of the Silverado repairs."

"We could make a cash offer with a time limit," said Norman. "It would be subject to selling our Wildwood Avenue fourplex in ninety days, and subject to our obtaining the necessary Silverado financing in ninety days."

"Ninety days is too long for the Benders to wait. But what would your cash price be?"

"$350,000," said Norman.

"That's impossible. Our $395,000 asking price is already a bargain."

THE WRIGHTS NEGOTIATE A THREE-WAY EXCHANGE AGREEMENT

Negotiations proceeded back and forth every day until the end of the week, Saturday, February 19, when the Wrights, the Benders, and the realtor concluded the following agreement.

The Benders were to receive a full price of $365,000, subject to their loan balance of $220,000. This gave them a credit of $145,000 in cash, from which they had to pay $25,000 in back taxes, other Silverado bills, and a 5 percent commission of $18,250 to Meeker & Mitchman Realtors.

The Wrights were to have sixty days to arrange refinancing of the Silverado, including improvement financing satisfactory to them. The Wrights also had sixty days to sell the Wildwood fourplex, to be listed exclusively with Meeker & Mitchman at a price of $245,000. The Wrights were to pay the realtors 5 percent of the sale price of Wildwood.

The realtors were to assist in securing financing for the Wrights, in addition to selling Wildwood. The Wildwood sale was to be handled as a three-way exchange for tax purposes so that the Wrights would owe no income taxes on their Wildwood profits. The Wrights would first deed the fourplex to the Benders in escrow and the Benders would then deed the property to the new buyers.

Within three weeks, by March 11, with the help of Meeker & Mitchman, the Wrights obtained the following loan commitments.

NEW WILDWOOD FOURPLEX LOAN

The maximum loan commitment obtained on the Wildwood fourplex was $220,000, payable in thirty years at $235 monthly, including 12½ percent interest. This loan required that the new owners live in one of the fourplex units.

INCREASING THE SILVERADO FIRST MORTGAGE

Meeker told the Wrights that the Capitol National Bank would make a second-mortgage rehabilitation loan to cover the Silverado repairs and improvements. They would accept second-loan position behind a first loan that did not exceed $260,000, the recorded amount of the present loan.

The Wrights figured it would be advantageous to raise extra cash by arranging with the present lenders, the Biggerts, to advance $40,000. This would bring their balance to $259,118, close to the original amount of $260,000, payable in thirty years. The Biggerts agreed, with the inducements of raising the interest overall from 8 to 9 percent and the payments from $1,908 to $2,092, including interest. The Biggerts stipulated that they must receive notices from the tax collector henceforth of any tax delinquencies.

THE BANK TAKES A SECOND MORTGAGE ON THE SILVERADO

At the Capitol National Bank the Wrights contacted Mr. Yeager, the real estate vice president who had handled the Paradise Apartments improvement loan. Yeager said that the Wrights' Silverado Apartments loan would qualify for the bank's new rehabilitation program. He turned the Wrights over to Mr. Dozer, newly appointed as rehabilitation officer.

Dozer looked over the Wrights' loan application and bank file. "I'm happy to see you have an excellent payment record," he said. "And it looks like you have plenty of equity to secure your rehabilitation loan. Of course, the bank has to appraise the property both before and after the work is completed. Our new rehabilitation program requires mandatory reserves and fees that must be added to your $92,580 contract."

Dozer listed the following charges:

Silverado Apartments rehabilitation contract	$ 92,580
Mandatory contractor's contingency reserve 10%	9,258
Total with contingency reserve	101,838
Mandatory bank reserve 5%	5,092
Total with contingency and bank reserve	106,930
Bank loan and appraisal fees 10% of above total	10,693
Builders control fee 1½% of contract, including contractor's reserve	1,528
Total loan	119,151

Dozer said that the interest would be 12 percent and the term fifteen years. All the funds except the bank reserve and fees would be deposited in a Builder's Control account when the escrow closed, and forty-five days later the Wrights would start paying $1,439 monthly including 12 percent interest.

Dozer mentioned that the bank customarily applied any unused portion of both the contractor's reserve and the bank reserve as credits against the loan principal when the work was completed.

Norman Wright protested, "That isn't fair, as you are charging us fees on all the funds. Any money left over should be deposited in our money market account here at the bank."

After some discussion Dozer agreed to Norman's request.

COMPLETING THE SILVERADO PURCHASE

A week later, on Saturday, March 19, Francis Meeker sold the Wildwood fourplex to the Youngs, with whom he had been dickering, at a price of $235,000. This sale and the sale of the Silverado were closed in escrow on Monday, March 28, with the following dispositions, in the Wrights' fourth purchase on their road to a million.

WILDWOOD SALE

1. As agreed, the Wrights deed Wildwood to the Benders and the Benders deed the fourplex to the Youngs, consummating a three-way exchange that is tax-free for the Wrights.
2. The Youngs deposit a cash down payment of $15,000 and take over the new Wildwood loan of $220,000.
3. The Wrights receive credit for the $15,000 down payment and the $220,000 loan funds, totaling $235,000. They pay off the existing loan balance of $76,866 and pay Meeker & Mitchman a 5 percent sales commission of $11,750. This leaves the Wrights with a net escrow credit from the Wildwood sale of $146,384.

SILVERADO PURCHASE

1. The lenders and previous owners, the Biggerts, deposit $40,000 in escrow. This is credited to the account of the Wrights, making their total escrow credits $186,384.
2. The Benders pay the $25,000 in back taxes plus the $18,250 sales commission from their $145,000 down payment escrow credit, giving them $101,750 in net cash for their disposal, including paying off other debts.
3. Meeker & Mitchman Realtors receives a total of $30,000 in sales fees for efforts in accomplishing a three-way exchange plus helping to develop creative financing.

4. Norman and Karen Wright credit their $145,000 cash down payment to the Benders, leaving the Wrights with net cash of $41,384 from the refinancing and exchange of the Wildwood fourplex for the Silverado Apartments.

5. The Wrights have a loan commitment from the bank to pay for all planned repairs and improvements with enough left over to pay them some additional cash from the reserve accounts. They are anxious to proceed with the fixer-upper work. When it is completed they expect their net worth to top a million.

THE SILVERADO TRANSFORMATION

By November 1, 1983, the Wrights have completed all projected repairs and improvements for the Silverado and have rented all apartments at or above their original estimate.

Rental income has paid the loan payments and expenses. After the Wrights assured them of prompt pay the Bolgers turned out to be competent managers and handled most of the maintenance and repairs. Although all the rents at least doubled, they appreciated having their apartment remain free of rent.

The managers readily rented the twenty 600-square-foot apartments converted from studios to one-bedrooms for the projected $360. The Wrights concluded that they should receive more for the eight original 800-square-foot one-bedroom apartments, so they were rented for $385 each. They rented the larger 960-square-foot one-bedroom apartment, number 215 above the manager, for $395. When they prepared a new operating statement the Wrights showed as gross income and offsetting management expense the same $395 amount for the managers' apartment, number 115, which also had 960 square feet.

The changes in rentals developed the following monthly income totals:

20 1-bedroom 600-square-foot apartments at
$360 each $7,200

8 1-bedroom 800-square-foot apartments at $385 each	3,080
2 1-bedroom 960-square-foot apartments at $395 each	790
20 garages at $10 each	200
Coin laundry income at 50 percent of gross	72
Total monthly income	$11,342
Total annual income	$136,104

The previously figured annual expenses were $20,449.22. Adding to this the $35 monthly increase to $395 for the free managers' apartment, number 115, made an annual increase of $420. This brought the revised annual expenses to $20,869.22, and the revised annual net income to $115,234,78. The revised capital value was $1,152,347.80.

The first mortgage was paid down to $258,089, and the second mortgage to $118,663, making the total loans $376,752. The Wrights' equity in the Silverado was $145,000 when purchased, representing their down payment. Their new equity after the transformation was $775,595.80, an increase of $630,595.80. This represented a fixer-upper profit of 601.7 percent or six times the improvement and financing costs of $104,801.

THE WRIGHTS' MILLIONAIRE FINANCIAL STATEMENT, NOVEMBER 1, 1983

The Wrights figured their complete investment statement as follows.

Estimated Equity in 30-unit Silverado Apartments $775,595
(Market value $1,152,347 less total loans $376,752)

Estimated Equity in 18-unit Paradise Apartments   401,729
(Market value $675,000 less total loans $273,271; 11 payments on the two loans

have reduced the principal on the first
mortgage to $152,827 and on the sec-
ond mortgage to $120,444.)

Money market balance   41,569
(December 10, 1982, balance of
$24,838 plus 10 percent interest for 11
months totals $27,219. In addition, Jack
Armstrong has completed the Silverado
fixer-upper work for his contracted price
of $92,580 and has not needed to draw
on the contingency reserves required by
the bank. As agreed, the bank deposits
the unused bank reserve of $5,092 and
contractor's reserve of $9,258 in the
Wrights' money market account, adding a total of $14,350.)

Credit union savings   7,017
(December 10, 1982, balance of $4,509
plus $200 monthly savings of $2,200
for 11 months, plus 6 percent interest
of $308)

Total net investment assets $1,225,910

Thirty-two months after buying the Spruce Street house the
Wrights have net investment assets of $1,225,910. In less than
three years they have topped a million and come very close to
equaling the five-year goal in Chapter 3 of $1,232,277.

CHAPTER 14

Carefree Semiretirement with Honest Property Managers

MANY REAL ESTATE investors, particularly part-time real estate investors with other businesses and professions demanding their full-time attention, may desire the benefits of income-property ownership without taking on the day-to-day responsibilities of on-site care and maintenance. This can be achieved to some extent through realty trusts and syndicates, where participants have little input in operating decisions and an average of 35 percent of a building's gross income is paid to outside management.

But you can also enjoy the benefits of individual real estate investment and still retain some control of money-making fixer-upper facilities by hiring a property manager, with management charges running an average of between 5 and 10 percent of gross income. Doctors, lawyers, and other professionals, along with full-time workers in a variety of fields, are turning to property managers in increasing numbers, handling operating details on even single-family rental homes.

Owners who seek help in managing their properties fall into four general groups: owners who, like myself, prefer to devote more time to other pursuits; owners who acquire more property than they can efficiently handle; owners who have been transferred out of town subsequent to their purchase; and, finally, other out-of-town owners, particularly owners of seasonal resort properties, who cannot personally be on hand to attend to daily business.

In most resort areas, a majority of the individual homeowners live out of town and offer their vacation homes for rent during peak seasons. Where do these owners turn to keep their seasonal rentals 100 percent full, and to take care of cleaning, maintenance and repairs, and other operating problems? To the local property managers, who customarily charge a reasonable 10 percent of the gross income on single-family homes for their valued service.

I have worked with several property managers and have interviewed dozens of prospects for the position. Add to this the hundreds of resident apartment managers I have employed to manage individual housing projects since 1940, and you'll recognize my broad and thorough experience in hiring on-site supervisory personnel.

Many books have been written on the various facets of property management, but advice is scarce on how to hire a property manager, someone to take the owner's place in a building's general supervision, including the hiring, firing, and supervising of resident managers and maintenance employees. That is the intent of this experience-based chapter.

LUCILLE SAYS, "SELL LA PERALTA"

I wanted to devote more time to encouraging others by writing, my first love among life's endeavors, and to lecturing at seminars and meetings, my second love. I decided to semiretire from property ownership and management, cutting drastically the time required for detailed supervision.

I sold about four hundred rental units, and still owned the hundred-unit La Peralta Apartments, the flagship of the various properties jointly held by my wife Lucille and me. Lucille wanted to cut loose from property supervision entirely by selling La

Peralta, so we could enjoy still more time for travel in addition to my writing and lecturing.

Underlying real estate precepts emphasized in my books, like maximum sound leveraging and improvement of properties, will always hold true, but tax applications and other details of investment conditions keep changing. I wanted to keep abreast of inevitable changes so I could continue to preach the up-to-date gospel of free enterprise through investing in fixer-upper real estate.

I enjoyed the opportunities for innovation and other challenges of property management, and also wanted to keep the tax advantages of some investment-property ownership. The continuing deductions for various tax credits, ongoing depreciation, and interest on loans looked mighty good when I wrote them down on my income tax returns.

How could I keep the enticing deductions and stop handling day-to-day management details? Real estate trusts and syndicates were ruled out because I wanted to keep in personal touch with new developments. I wanted to retain the right to make my own final decisions on major improvements and ongoing policies. The ideal solution to the apparent dilemma of choosing owner management or selling out was to retain ownership and semiretire from supervision by hiring a property manager. This solution also gave me an opportunity to learn more at first hand about a field apart from actual management—the advantages and problems of supervising property managers.

VALOR VS. DISCRETION

Management is a highly competitive and growing field, and I have had experience with both good and bad representatives. I have learned something from every property manager contact. One disappointing property manager whom I had to fire taught me the necessity of tighter safeguards against dishonesty!

One never knows when personality clashes or disagreeable experiences may make a change necessary. If I named good managers and omitted bad ones, I'd risk the accusation of damning by omission, so all names in this chapter, as in most of this book, will be fictitious. All characters will be composites and no cited character is intended to depict any actual person. I will quote pertinent clauses recommended for a property management contract, but with names changed.

GREAT EXPECTATIONS

An alert owner expects a competent property manager to take over most details of supervision, keep honest records, and make honest reports. All this, and to wind up with a higher net income for each property than the owner would probably have. How? By constant application of the two great, ever-recurring levers for increasing net bankable income:

1. Increase gross income.
2. Decrease expenses.

A good property manager welcomes the opportunity to make improvements that increase values and therefore increase rental income, which the property manager shares proportionately.

I have found, to my delighted surprise, that aggressive, competent property managers move faster than most owners at maintaining rents closer to the top of an upsurging market. In many cases they produce a greater net income *after paying property management fees* than the average hesitant owner would earn on his own, lagging below the market. Thus I have wound up with more operating income from La Peralta after semiretiring than before. It is no detraction from this feat of management to add that I have plowed all the net income into continuing improvements to the sturdy but aging La Peralta, built, as mentioned, in 1908, soon after the great earthquake.

FALSE STARTS

I made several false starts in choosing a competent and honest property manager. I answered newspaper ads and promotional letters offering to make an owner rich and carefree by providing experienced property managers with a golden touch for making money. Most of the advertisers were small real estate brokers looking primarily for listings to sell property, with the inducement of management a stepping-stone. They expected a knowledgeable owner to teach them how to operate his property. Many charged exorbitant fees, up to 25 percent, for little responsibility.

I contacted some nationally known realtors who handled major sales and leases and operated property management divisions. The actual property managers referred to me were mostly young beginners just graduated from college with a degree in business administration. They had taken a course or two in real estate sales and appraisal, but they had little or no schooling, from college or boss, in property management.

They visualized their role as mainly picking up monthly income-and-expense reports from resident managers, who were expected to perform most of the duties of property management. The property manager furnished the owner with copies of the resident manager's reports, along with net income checks, if any, after deducting healthy management fees.

Where a good property manager welcomes improvements, most would-be property managers shun the supervision of any major improvements. They expect the owner to continue with such supervision or hire an architect or general contractor to do the supervising. They typically demand a minimum bonus of 10 percent of the contract cost if they undertake the supervision of any such major improvements.

IT TAKES ONE TO KNOW ONE

I asked several realtor friends who were not themselves into property management if they could recommend a firm which performed more than simple bookkeeping and would diligently handle improvements. I expected to participate in overall planning and financing of improvements on a continuing basis.

Three realtors recommended the same firm, Fixer Uppers management, a company which specialized in following my suggestions. It took over run-down apartments owned by neglectful or unimaginative owners, fixed the properties up on a concentrated continuing program, and usually made them ready for resale within six months at a big profit. Fixer Upper turned over the buying and selling of properties to other realtors, and earned a bonus by sharing the realtor's sales fees.

I said, "That's the firm for me."

Many property managers demand a percentage of contract costs or a bonus for preparing a property for resale. The quickest way for an investor to build a substantial estate is by continuous improvement and turnover, as practiced by the Wrights and advocated by Fixer Upper. Those investors interested in sustained ownership for indefinite periods, as I am after pyramiding as far as I want in property holdings, can experience a continuing increase in income and value by making ongoing improvements.

It certainly pays to investigate a property manager's attitude toward improvements. Most management firms don't want to undertake any task that consumes more than minimum supervisory and reporting time. Even though all rent raises increase the management compensation on a percentage basis, some poor management firms resist any raises, as this may result in some vacancies taking a little more time to fill.

EQUAL OPPORTUNITY

I phoned the Fixer Upper office and made an appointment with the manager, Mrs. Moira Pride. I pointed out to her that planned improvements at La Peralta would both increase existing rents and create new rentals. Each improvement step would increase value and therefore increase income. Doubled overall rents would double the property manager's income.

"I love fixing up properties and increasing the income," commented Mrs. Pride. "I've stepped in behind a lazy, do-nothing property manager who was afraid to raise rents, and I've succeeded in doubling the rents in a few months' time."

She said that she would relish the challenge of working with me on a continuing basis to make as many profitable improvements as possible to enhance the quaint and elderly Peralta. She loved its location near the lake and close to downtown. Some management firms charged a minimum fee of 10 percent of the gross income. For an operation as big as La Peralta she would take over the property management for 6 percent of the gross income. She asked for no extra fees for supervising improvements, as she realized that any sensible improvements would automatically result in higher income and higher fees.

I said, "The previous property manager, Mr. Grundle, supervised improvements, although not as efficiently as expected. He charged 5 percent. This should be adequate, as the income keeps growing. I believe in equal opportunity and equal pay for men and women, and I expect to pay you the same 5 percent that I paid before. But not a bonus for changing from unattractive male to attractive female supervision!"

Mrs. Pride laughingly agreed to 5 percent. She said she was a divorcée who had to support two children. After all, any contract, like marriage, was subject to trial and, if unsatisfactory to either party, to future cancellation. Details of our contract follow, with occasional interruptions and comments.

PROFESSIONAL MANAGEMENT AGREEMENT

In consideration of the covenants herein contained, W. E. Nickerson, hereinafter called Owner, and Fixer Upper Management Company, hereinafter called Agent, agree as follows:

1. The Owner employs the Agent exclusively to rent, lease, operate, and manage the property known as La Peralta Apartments, 184 13th Street, Oakland, CA 94612, consisting of 94 residential units and 6 commercial units, making a total of 1000 [rental] units; upon the terms hereinafter set forth, for the period of two (2) years beginning on this 1st day of July, 1982, and terminating the 30th day of June, 1984, which is the final and complete termination date of this contract; provided, however, that this contract shall be extended for one year on each 1st day of July unless either party gives to the other party a 30-day written notice to terminate; and provided that either party hereto may terminate this contract effective the 30th day of any month during any year prior to or after such final termination date, by giving to the other party a 30-day notice in writing of an intention to so terminate.

2. The Agent accepts the employment and agrees:

a. To use diligence in the management of the premises for the period and upon the terms herein provided, and agrees to furnish the services of its organization for the renting leasing, operating, and managing of the herein described premises.

b. To render monthly statements of receipts, expenses and charges and to remit to Owner receipts less disbursements. In the event the disbursements shall be in excess of the rents collected by the Agent, the Owner hereby agrees to pay such excess promptly upon demand of the Agent. Each statement entry for supplies, furnishings, equipment, or other materials shall be accompanied by a detailed invoice, showing vendor's name and address, the delivery address, and the signature of an authorized employee who receives delivery.

SAFEGUARDS FOR HONESTY

When their statements showed only a charge and a billing name, with no invoice, some property managers have billed several owners for the same delivery. Each item on a statement should be backed by an invoice, which should itemize each different purchase and show the name, address, and telephone number of the supplier, in case you wish to contact the supplier for any corroboration.

Each invoice should show the delivery address and signature of an authorized employee, workman, tenant, or other person who received delivery. This discourages a dishonest employee from claiming that the goods were never received.

Some property managers accustomed to providing only a statement with no invoices may protest about the nuisance. But the safeguard of detailed invoices should be insisted upon. If necessary, the owner should seek a more cooperative property manager.

Another important reason to insist on detailed invoices is the Internal Revenue Service. I have found that a knowledgeable revenue agent making a thorough audit is apt to ask for certain invoices at random as proof that all statement items are backed by authentic invoices. If requested invoices are produced the agent may decide to shorten his audit and pass up other possible lines of inquiry. If a requested invoice is not available the agent may challenge a whole group of associated deductions, and may decide to make a more extensive and time-consuming audit than first planned.

Let's continue with the details of my contractual agreement with Fixer Upper:

> c. To deposit all receipts collected for Owner, less any sums properly deducted or otherwise provided for herein, in a trust account in a national or state institution qualified to engage in the banking or trust business, entirely separate from Agent's personal account or the accounts of other Owners.

An agent who commingled accounts spent a considerable amount of the owner's funds for personal use, then went bankrupt. The agent went to jail. But remaining commingled funds were frozen by the bankruptcy court as part of the agent's assets, against which the owner could file his claim but with little or no likelihood of much recovery.

> d. Agent's employees who handle or are responsible for Owner's monies shall be bonded by a fidelity bond in an adequate amount.
>
> 3. The Owner hereby gives to the Agent the following authority and powers and agrees to assume the expenses in connection herewith:
>
> a. To advertise the availability for rental of the herein described premies or any part thereof, and to display "For Rent" and "Managed by" signs thereon; to sign, renew and/or cancel leases for the premises or any part thereof in the name of Fixer Upper Management Company as lessor; to collect rents and other charges and expenses due or to become due and give receipts therefor; to terminate tenancies and to sign and serve in the name of the Owner or in the name of Fixer Upper Management Company as lessor such notices as are appropriate; to institute and prosecute actions and to evict tenants and to recover possession of said premises and to sue for in the name of Fixer Upper Management Company or of the Owner and recover rents and other sums due; and when expedient, to settle, compromise, and release such actions or suits or reinstate such tenancies. Any lease executed for the Owner by the Agent shall not exceed one (1) year except with the specific consent of the Owner.
>
> b. To make contracts for electricity, gas, fuel, water, telephone, window cleaning, rubbish hauling, and other services or such of them as the Agent shall deem advisable; the Owner to assume the obligation of any contract so entered into at the termination of the agreement.
>
> c. To pay Social Security payroll taxes and Unemployment and Worker's Compensation Insurance. The Agent is hereby directed to accrue and pay for same from the Owner's funds.
>
> d. To pay mortgage indebtedness, property taxes, and the following insurance when so directed by the Owner. The

Owner will handle mortgage payments, property taxes, and the following insurance until further notice.

(1) Insurance for the perils of fire, lightning, wind, hail, explosion, smoke, riot, aircraft, vehicles, vandalism, and burglary on the contents in the amount of $100,000.00.

(2) "All Risk" protection on the building and rental income in the amount of $3,000,000.00 on the building and 100 percent on rental income.

(3) Insurance for comprehensive liability for personal injury and property damage in the amount of $1,000,000.00.

WHO PAYS THE BILLS?

The property manager expects to collect all income and pay all bills, including all repairs and minor improvements. However, there are some bills that the property manager may pay or the owner may handle, as I do. Some owners prefer that the property manager take care of all billing, including the financing of major improvements, plus all the so-called fixed or ongoing charges, like property taxes and licenses, loan payments, and insurance.

In this case the property manager usually earmarks a monthly reserve to pay for annual or semiannual charges, like taxes and insurance. The property manager may also order insurance to replace any that expires. I prefer to handle these payments, insurance orders, and any reserve requirements myself. This gives me better control of reserve funds, which I can deposit in accounts that pay the highest interest. I can be sure the required loan, insurance, and tax payments are made when due. More than one busy property manager has allowed these necessary payments to become delinquent, causing blemishes to otherwise spotless owner credit records. Also, I can be sure of competitive bids, without kickbacks to the property manager, when insurance is due for renewal.

On with the contract:

> e. To hire, discharge, and supervise the labor and employees required for the operation and maintenance of the premises;

it being agreed that all employees shall be deemed employees of Fixer Upper Management Company and that their compensations drawn from the building trustee account shall include the employer compensations as required by law as well as the pro-rata share of the Worker's Compensation Insurance carried by Fixer Upper Management Company; it being further agreed that the Agent may perform any of its duties through the Owner's attorneys, agents, or employees, as well as its employees, and shall not be responsible for their acts, defaults, or negligence if reasonable care has been exercised by Agent.

WHO FILES PAYROLL RECORDS?

Note that all building employees are required to be employees of the property manager. This helps assure that the property manager will handle all payroll records and reports. I have found that many property managers refuse to maintain the payroll of building employees, like the resident manager and maintenance people. They avoid filing the necessary Social Security, Unemployment Insurance, and Worker's Compensation reports.

I insist on this significant requirement that separates the all-inclusive take-charge pros from the limited-responsibility amateurs. The property manager should be responsible for all employee contacts, like hiring, firing, paychecks, and supervision, and for all necessary payroll reports.

About the only remaining government-required papers that the owner is usually responsible for filing are federal, state, and local income tax returns.

And, concluding with the contract:

f. To make or cause to be made and supervise maintenance services, repairs, and alterations, and to do decorating and rehabilitation on said premises; to purchase supplies and pay all bills therefor. The Agent agrees to secure the prior approval of the Owner on all expenditures in excess of $1,000.00

for any one item, except monthly or recurring operating charges and/or emergency repairs in excess of the maximum if in the option of the Agent such repairs are necessary to protect the property from damage or prevent damage to the property or person of others or to avoid suspension of necessary services or to avoid penalties or fines or to maintain services to the tenants as called for in their leases/agreements.

4. The Owner further agrees:

a. For Management to pay the Agent 5 percent of gross collected rents;

b. For Late Charge Collections to pay the Agent 5 percent;

c. For deposit collections no charge;

d. For leasing no charge;

e. For modernization no charge;

f. For refinancing not applicable;

g. For fire restoration no charge;

h. For undertaking work exceeding that usual to normal management, such as major rehabilitation, obtaining income tax advice, presenting petitions to planning or zoning committees, or other counseling, no charge will apply unless a fee for such services is agreed upon before any such work begins.

i. To idemnify and save the Agent completely harmless from any and all costs, expenses, attorney's fees, suits, liabilities, damages or claims for damages, including but not limited to those arising out of any injury or death to any person or persons or damages to any property of any kind whatsoever and to whomsoever belonging, including Owner, in any way relating to the management of the premises by the Agent or the performance or exercise of any of the duties, obligations, powers, or authorities herein or hereafter granted to the Agent; to carry, at Owner's sole cost and expense, such Public Liability, Property Damage, and Worker's Compensation Insurance as shall be adequate to protect the interests of the Agent and Owner, the policies for which shall name the Agent as well as the Owner as the party insured. The Agent shall not be liable for any error or judgment or for any mistake of fact or law, or for anything which it may do or refrain from doing, except in cases of willful misconduct or gross negligence.

5. This Management Agreement shall be binding upon the heirs, administrators, executors, successors, and assigns of the Owner and of the Agent.

6. If it shall become necessary for Agent or Owner to give notice of any kind to each other, the same shall be given, and shall be complete, by personal delivery or by sending such notice by registered or certified mail to the address shown under their signatures.

Agreed to this 1st day of July, 1982, at Oakland, Alameda County, California.

W̶E̶ ̶N̶i̶c̶k̶e̶r̶s̶o̶n̶   *Moira Pride*

W. E. NICKERSON, OWNER   MOIRA PRIDE, MANAGER

LA PERALTA   FIXER UPPER MANAGE-
APARTMENTS   MENT COMPANY
184 13th Street   1107 Liberty Avenue
Oakland, California 94612   Oakland, California 94610

AN OFFER THEY CAN'T REFUSE

To a couple seeking to lower their living expenses and to provide a little extra something for their growing nest egg, the chance to work as an apartment or property manager is often too good to pass up.

I know of one husband who returned home from his nine-to-five job one afternoon to share the exciting news of this new job opportunity with his wife.

"I've got this great job lined up," he said. "It pays a good salary, paid holidays and vacation, and free rent, including all utilities."

"That's wonderful," his wife replied.

"I knew you'd be pleased," the husband said. "You start on Monday as an apartment manager."

CHAPTER 15

Effective Management in Today's Market

Now that I had a property manager in place, it was up to me to train her in the management system of my design. And Mrs. Moira Pride proved her eagerness and willingness to learn my way of doing business by asking early on how I made millions by curing sick, run-down properties.

"Please advise me on some of your conclusions," Mrs. Pride asked. "What are some of the latest money-saving trends?"

KEEP LOOKING FOR IMPROVEMENTS

Every property operation needs periodic examination by the owner and the property manager, looking for profitable improvements. Dramatic surgery may be required to turn a sick apartment house from a money-loser into a healthy profit-maker.

It is well to keep reiterating the essentials of property management, sometimes lost in a forest of operating details. What is the fundamental purpose of improving operations? To make a greater net profit. This involves two basic goals: maximum gross income and minimum expenses. Some management decisions cover one or the other. Some affect both. For example, modern-

189

izing with new plumbing can increase rents and at the same time decrease repair bills.

How can you increase rents and reduce expenses? There are two major remedies. They are profitable improvements, as undertaken by the Wrights and described in previous chapters, and effective management, to be outlined in this chapter.

CURING VACANCIES

Apartments generally are running fairly full now, primarily because of slackened new construction. But our general market is always competitive, and in some projects the biggest destroyer of gross income is a high vacancy factor. Whereas a well-run, established building can be 100 percent full, a brand-new structure starts out 100 percent vacant. It takes several months to reverse from all-vacant to all-occupied. Experienced owners help cure vacancies in a new building by paying bonuses to top managers.

A survey of higher-priced new properties in operation for at least six months shows an average vacancy factor of a discouraging 20 percent. A similar red-ink percentage may apply to older properties that are allowed to run down till they are no longer competitive.

IMPORTANCE OF APARTMENT MANAGERS

The most important single secret of successful apartment investment is often a competent, cooperative resident manager. A good, personable manager is needed on the premises whether the property is supervised by the owner or other overall management.

Some resident managers consider themselves chiefly spokesman for the tenants. Others ride the fence as referees between owner and tenants. The ideal manager, however, always operates in the best interests of the owner. Every resident manager and property manager should be guided by this question: "What would I do if I owned the building myself?"

When you inspect a building as a prospective buyer it pays to appraise the resident manager and the premises at the same time. Go over the rent roll with the manager in his or her office or apartment, then insist that the manager accompany you in looking over individual apartments. A smart resident manager will know he or she is on trial whenever a prospective buyer comes to inspect the building.

Observe whether or not the resident manager knows the job and is filling it efficiently and pleasantly. Is the building almost full? Are rent collections up to date? Are vacancies clean and ready to rent? Is the manager grumpy or cooperative with you? Are tenants pleased with the resident manager's attitude? How does he or she handle personal contacts and telephone calls?

While I was in one resident manager's office a prospective renter called for directions, a common occurrence in the day-to-day life of any manager. But this manager answered as though she were being asked the question for the first time.

"You can't miss it," she said. "It's a big white building." That's all she said, and then she hung up. Of course, a manager should always give clear and complete directions. For all I know that one tenant prospect could still be driving around town, looking for a big white building with a vacancy sign.

Some resident managers prove very desirable, and you will want to keep them. If you find a building with many vacancies and delinquent tenants, there may be several reasons. Very often the main problem is a poor manager. Perhaps the former owner hired an ineffective relative. Or a previously efficient manager has not kept up with competition, and has grown sloppy with age and indifference. Or the manager is just not cut out for the job. Some managers make you wonder how an owner or property manager could possibly have hired them.

WAITING FOR ST. PETER

In my travels I met one sorry example of a resident manager who happened to be an elderly aunt of the owner. A mop of bleached-blond hair hung in strings over her shoulders and down her food-stained dress. She refused to clean or show vacant apartments. She let garbage accumulate for new tenants to clean out. She kept her door on a burglarproof chain, and if a prospective tenant came along she just poked a key out the crack. Rents were far below market levels, but the building was half empty.

"Why don't you show the apartments?" I asked the old woman. "You're bound to rent more if you go with prospective tenants and try to sell them."

She replied, "I'm seventy-four years old and stayed a virgin up to now. I intend to stay pure till I go through the Pearly Gates. I'm not going to give any nasty man a chance to rape me. I'm saving myself for St. Peter."

Incidentally, this unqualified manager inadvertently helped me to buy the twenty-four unit building at about half the going market. Her very presence, and the fact that she wasn't doing her job, decreased the market value of the building she represented. On taking possession I arranged a thorough cleanup and hired a young, attractive, and competent resident manager. She filled the building at doubled rents within one month.

SEXY BLONDE

I know of a different problem involving the resident manager of a large country-club apartment complex. She was a sexy blond of twenty-five whose Air Force husband was overseas. She liked sunbathing by the swimming pool in a topless bikini at midday. Some of the tenant women complained because their husbands made special trips home for lunch and a swim at noon.

The manager seldom came to the door at all in the afternoons when prospective tenants called. Why? Because she was sleeping with the gardener. This not only meant that she didn't rent apartments or collect rents during a normally productive time. It also meant that the yard got full of weeds. The gardener was doing plenty of cultivating, but in the wrong bed!

If there is obvious incompetence, don't make the mistake of

taking over the resident manager when you buy a property. Then you or your property manager have to fire her. Make this unpleasant task the responsibility of the seller. Arrange to have your own new manager take over at the same time you assume ownership.

WHERE TO FIND GOOD MANAGERS?

Where will you or your property manager find a good resident manager? Many property managers maintain a roster of competent resident managers, who usually start with smaller properties and are anxious to move up to larger complexes. If you are fortunate your local Apartment Association will also have a list of good managers, as many associations train and place managers. There are bound to be jewels among them, especially those who have taken the worthwhile training sponsored by the Apartment Association.

If a suitable resident manager is not available from the management or association pools, you might check if any of the present tenants wants the job and is qualified. Tenants who fill your requirements can work out very well as managers. Like the tenants who bought the Spruce Street house, they already like the accommodations and neighborhood or they wouldn't be paying rent.

Or you can get a good manager by putting a small ad in the newspaper under "Couple Wanted" or a similar heading. Some single men or women can do a good job, but couples usually work out best and stay on longer. You might want to hire both husband and wife full-time to run a complex of forty apartments or more. Or, especially with fewer units, you could allow one partner to work an outside job while the other remains on-site to show or rent apartments, collect and bank the rents, supervise maintenance people, perform routine maintenance chores and minor repair work, and arrange to clean vacancies and community areas.

PERMANENT MANAGERS

Resident managers should be hired with the expectation that they will stay with you several years .after you have trained them in your way of operating. But I always recommend a written contract specifying that they are originally hired for a trial period, and that they may quit or be discharged on thirty days' notice.

To avoid burglaries or robberies, resident managers should be instructed to accept no cash but only money orders or checks for the amount of rent and deposits due, and to give no change. A notice of this effect should be posted in the manager's office or apartment along with a notice stating the dire consequences of giving a bad check.

It should be put in writing that managers are responsible for any losses from giving change for bad checks. This usually stops giving change. The owner is responsible for bad-check losses applied to rents, but not for change. That way you don't have extra losses from the bad-check artists who are out to cheat you.

One that I know of handed over a phony "paycheck" for $550 to pay the $450 rent and deposits on an apartment. He sweet-talked the manager into giving him $100 change. He said he wanted to move in right away. Instead he went on down the street to the next gullible manager.

Because they are anxious to rent an apartment, it is easy for managers to be talked into giving the owner's money away in change. But a manager seldom gives out his or her own money. That's one difference between soft and hard money. It's hard money if it comes out of your own pocket!

TRIPLICATE LEASES

You should always have a written lease or rental agreement for each tenancy. Property managers maintain a complete supply of leases and other forms. Usually such supplies are also available through your Apartment Association. The house rules and an inventory of furnishings should be included. Usually a tenant will readily sign a rental agreement if the manager presents it as a matter of course before turning over the keys. If you give up the keys, then hand a tenant the lease to study afterward, he is more apt to raise objections. Never give anyone the keys to an apartment until after the rent and all required deposits are paid and the lease signed.

It helps keep the manager honest and prevent losses if leases and inventories are prepared in triplicate. One copy goes to the tenant, one to the resident manager, and one to the owner or property manager. A triplicate lease on file verifies when an apartment is rented, when the rent starts, the amount of rent and deposits, and the number of tenants.

The lease may be only month-to-month, but it should spell out legally allowable terms that give the owner the upper hand in case a tenant proves troublesome or a deadbeat. For example, the manager should be able to show an apartment after a vacate notice is given, and should be able to hold personal belongings as security if the tenant fails to pay rent. An ironclad lease gives no problem to a tenant who pays his rent on time and behaves decently. It should be an effective weapon over the deadbeat, the troublemaker, and the outright crook.

GIVING NOTICES

It is a common practice to provide for a thirty-day notice to change a lease. The tenant may give a thirty-day notice to vacate. The owner may give a thirty-day notice of eviction or of a change in terms, such as a rent raise. The thirty-day period conforms with most state laws, as in California, on monthly rentals, unless you have an agreement to the contrary.

However, you might consider a written agreement specifying a fifteen-day notice from both parties, which I prefer because it is easier to enforce. For example, if a tenant has a sudden job transfer he may readily give notice and pay up for a fifteen-day period. But thirty days might be enough of a burden to encourage his skipping out without any notice.

It's an advantage for the owner to be able to give a fifteen-day notice for raises or other changes. For example, if the rent is due on the first of the month and the tenant happens to pay on the second or third, a thirty-day notice given on those days would not be effective the first of the following month. But a fifteen-day notice allows plenty of leeway. It can be given as late as the sixteenth day of a thirty-day month and still be effective the first of the following month, making raises due one month earlier. This can result in a sizable increase in revenue at the end of the year if you are following a continuing program of profit-making improvements accompanied by rent raises.

A shorter notice also speeds up either an outright eviction or making a substantial raise in order to influence a tenant to move. If you give a straightforward eviction notice, an undesirable tenant may fight it and prolong his vacating. Unless there are rent controls, there is not much a tenant can do about a raise except pay it or move.

SUPERVISING THE RESIDENT MANAGER

As mentioned, the resident manager should collect the rents only by money order or check in order to avoid the trauma and losses of burglary or robbery. A no-cash policy also helps discourage fidelity losses. I know of spendthrift managers who have skipped to Mexico after accumulating substantial amounts of cash. But you don't see much skipping when there is little or no cash to skip with!

The manager should deposit receipts at least once a week in the nearest bank where the owner has an account. Have the bank give a duplicate receipt to the manager and mail a copy to the owner or property manager. After checking in a new resident manager, the owner or property manager should make a supervisory visit not less than once a week for the first month or so to go over the books and operations.

Managers appreciate having a certain independence and responsiblity. After a month or so, unless there are unusual problems, the owner or property manager should go on a regular schedule for experienced managers of a one-to-two hour supervisory visit every two weeks.

The manager should make out a balance sheet every time a banking transaction is conducted. This form shows income collected and authorized incidental expenses paid out, like refunds of key deposits. At all times the manager is subject to audit. For every dollar collected the money must be on hand or accounted for by bank deposit slips or receipts for expenditures.

The resident manager also makes out a report of total income on a monthly basis. This shows by apartment number each tenant's name, number of tenants, amount of scheduled and collected rent, when due and when collected, and any extra charges due and collected for extra items like key, security, and damages deposits.

The manager should be encouraged to ask questions and make suggestions, to which the owner or property manager should be open-minded. The manager should be given praise when due.

KEEP INSPECTING

In addition to checking the bookkeeping and other operations, it pays to inspect all vacancies on each supervisory visit. An honest manager wants the owner or property manager to see the vacancies in order to help rent them. Incidentally, this prevents the resident manager from reporting as vacant an apartment that is already rented and pocketing the money, or from filling a "vacant" apartment with freeloading relatives. You know, with today's fast travel, there is no such thing as a distant relative!

Where supervisors have not routinely inspected all vacancies, some managers close to motels have delayed bona fide renting and rented vacancies to overflow transient tenants over weekends, keeping the money.

The chief purposes of regular inspection by the owner or property manager are to verify that apartments are clean and ready to show to prospective tenants. Look for profitable improvements that can be made, like those described in Chapters 5 and 7. Only minor changes may be needed to make an apartment more rentable, like painting, paneling one wall, or changing furniture. Sometimes merely rearranging existing furniture can make a big difference. Sometimes new furniture needs to be added, or perhaps new drapes, or just an eye-catching item like a painting or new lamp.

If the manager has shown an apartment at least three times to qualified prospects and not rented, then usually something needs correction. Possibly the rent should be lowered. This might be considered an added attraction, especially for the least-desirable unit where several similar apartments are vacant. Lowering the rent should be the last step for consideration. After all, the general rent trend continues upward. You have to raise rents at least 5 percent a year, sometimes up to 10 percent, just to keep up with increasing costs. Rather than lower rents, it is much more profitable to spend a little money on improvements, then increase rents.

100 PERCENT MAY BE A BAD SIGN

A 100 percent full building, with hardly any turnover except by death, used to be considered a sign of good management. On an ever rising market it may indicate poor management that has allowed rents to coast at low, low levels. This kind of situation is apt to prevail under absentee or heirloom ownership. It presents a ready-made opportunity for the fixer-upper buyer willing to modernize and improve the property and the management.

If a vacancy or two initially results from raising the rents, the increased income should still give a bigger profit. For example, a ten-unit building full at $200 per unit means $2,000 monthly. The same building at $400 per unit with one vacancy equals $3,600 monthly.

KEEP SELLING

Inspection and discussion may reveal that an apartment is in good condition and the rent competitive, but the unit stays vacant far too long because of poor salesmanship. The manager may need to improve his or her technique of showing and selling apartments. Desirable items like an attractive view, new drapes, or a modern electric kitchen should be pointed out. I actually heard one manager say, "This is the living room. This is the kitchen. There's the bath." And nothing more to sell an apartment!

There's no use trying to sell an obviously unsuitable or dissatisfied prospect, but many good prospects slip away because good points are not mentioned, or nobody invites them to rent or pay a holding deposit.

If there is a question about the manager's technique—and there should be if vacant and readied apartments remain unrented—it pays to review their methods. You might suggest an extension course in salesmanship, which you should consider paying for, or you might refer the manager to any of a long list of books and pamphlets on the art of selling in general and of selling and renting apartments in particular. If a manager is acceptable in other areas of the job you should do everything you can to train him or her in the desired method of showing and renting apartments. It is sometimes worth the extra effort to keep an honest and otherwise competent manager on the job.

HOW TO SELL AN APARTMENT

Let's cover some of the basics of showing and renting vacant apartments. To begin with, you should always point out some particular advantage in each room. It's important not to state the obvious, like the manager above, but to aggressively accentuate what the prospective tenants can plainly see. For example, comments such as "This furnace really throws out the heat in a hurry when you want it" and "The master bedroom is plenty large enough even for twin beds" help to get your prospect thinking of an apartment's ability to meet his unique needs.

Try to turn obvious objections into not-so-obvious appeals. If a prospect protests that a walk-up apartment is on the top floor, point out that top-floor tenants are not subjected to noise from the apartment above. And don't draw attention to an apartment's obvious disadvantages; although you want to be honest in your dealings with all prospects, you should let an apartment's drawbacks speak for themselves. Besides, what may appear disadvantageous to the owner or the manager may not loom as a large obstacle to an individual tenant.

You'd be surprised at the number of apartments that remain vacant simply because interested prospects haven't been specifically asked to rent. Sure, the prospect is there because he's looking for a place to live, and he knows you're there showing him the apartment to fill a vacancy, but most people won't act on their interest until you come right out and invite them to buy. I advocate two simple methods for asking prospects to buy— one, the "direct request" method; and two, the "left-handed request" method.

THE DIRECT REQUEST

Some prospects are so eager to rent they make a cursory inspection of the premises, then turn to the manager and say, "I'll take it." But most people wait to be asked, and the best way of asking is by making a direct request: "Would you like to take the apartment?"

Of course, this is the easiest and, as its name implies, most direct approach, but it does often result in unnecessary failure. Many tenants like to spar before making up their minds. Unfortunately, it's too easy to say no to a direct question, and once a hasty no is rendered, it's extremely difficult to turn it into a yes.

THE LEFT-HANDED REQUEST

The easist way to encourage a positive response from your prospect is to get him or her to back into a positive answer through a "contained decision" line of questioning. You'll find it most effective to ask an indirect, or "left-handed," question such as "When can you move in?" or "We're repainting that wall over there—what color would you prefer?" Couched in the prospect's response will be an indirect intention to buy.

Many lines of inquiry can be employed for this type of request, covering alternative choice of accommodations ("Would you prefer an apartment with a garbage disposal?"), payment and lease arrangements ("Would you like to look over our lease, in case you have any questions?"), and the availability of parking spaces ("The space in the middle is available, but the one on the end is opening up next week and might be more convenient. What do you think?").

FRESHEN ADVERTISING

To help managers sell apartments, owners should do their part by advertising to get prospects to the premises. Lighted signs help. So do well-kept grounds, which in many cases can be the best advertising available to you. Ads in service magazines help to draw service personnel. Newspaper classified ads usually produce the best results, but it's important not to allow your ads to grow stale. Freshen the wording about once a week by varying your key word ("Spacious!" "Sunny!") and attention-getting appeals.

Does your project cater to certain types of tenants? Your advertising should be slanted to draw those most suited to your vacancies. Many successful apartments cater to special groups with similar interests, such as senior citizens, families with children, newlyweds, and young singles. Of course, each group desires special amenities, such as community recreation and card rooms, playgrounds, swimming pools, and saunas.

After location and price, which are already known to the prospective tenant, service is the number-one demand of most tenants. The manager should emphasize willingness to serve when showing apartments. Security is also a major consideration, closely followed by convenience and recreation, a friendly manager, and congenial neighbors.

HOW TO SCREEN CONGENIAL TENANTS WHO WILL PAY THEIR RENTS

I am often asked, "How do you screen your tenants?"

Each prospective tenant fills out a written application, showing credit and character references. Most property managers and Apartment Associations have such forms, along with many others previously mentioned.

The written application not only helps to screen out undesirables and select congenial tenants who will pay their rents. It also lists names and addresses of close relatives and friends you can notify if the tenant becomes ill or dies. And it tells you where to locate a tenant who does skip out owing rent.

The resident manager should initially screen prospective tenants. If their income is sufficient to pay the rent and they appear otherwise suitable, they should then be checked with a credit bureau. Some lazy managers refer all prospects to a credit bureau without any preliminary screening. This is a waste of time and money, even though the referral fee is reasonable, when the manager's own prior screening may indicate undesirability.

The manager should first make a preliminary verification of employment and of satisfactory tenancy at the present rental and the previous rental. The latter rental reference is most important and more apt to be honest about rent-paying and other habits. The owner or manager of a present rental may give a good report in order to hasten the departure of an undesirable tenant.

One prospect said, "I'll just take this little old application along and have my free lawyer at Legal Aid look it over before I sign it."

The manager should not let the reference form leave the building. The tenant must fill it out and leave it with the manager, just like an application for employment. Otherwise the prospective tenant is no longer a prospect.

When interviewing manager applicants, have both husband and wife fill out this same reference form if you seriously consider hiring them. The credit and character information helps to make a final choice among several qualified applicants.

If properly handled, the reference form helps give the owner and manager absolute discretion in selecting tenants. Regardless of other factors, if you don't approve prospective tenants' looks or attitudes, you can turn them down because you do not okay their character and credit references. This helps you select tenants who are more apt to find their neighbors congenial.

HOLDING GOOD TENANTS

Factors that prospective tenants desire are also important to keep in mind, to help hold good tenants. A tenant who stays reduces repair and decorating bills. One survey shows noise a main cause of moving. How can you improve soundproofing at reasonable cost? Look at the floors, ceilings, and walls.

If the ceilings are high enough you can provide sound-deadening air space with a drop ceiling. If space is limited you can install acoustical tile at low cost. A big sound deadener between floors is rubber padding under wall-to-wall carpet. An added course of Sheetrock or paneling, especially if furred out to create an air space, can deaden noise between walls.

Some tenants, particularly if they are moving to smaller quarters, like empty nesters from a house to a less spacious apartment, have an insatiable demand for additional surplus storage. They must have a place for keepsakes they just cannot part with. They can't fit all their treasured belongings into their small apartment, where you have already provided maximum feasible storage space. How to solve the problem? Consider meeting this growing need by converting dead-storage areas in the basement and/or attic into various-sized individual mini-storage spaces, with good security locks and ample lighting. This solution at La Peralta, as covered in Chapter 8, has made many old and new tenants happy by providing all the storage they want at nominal cost.

YES, YOU CAN INSURE FIDELITY!

Regardless of safeguards against losses, it usually pays to cover all resident managers and any other handlers of your funds with fidelity insurance, which costs very little. I hired one young couple and told them all my managers were covered by a blanket fidelity policy. The husband was a long-distance truck driver, and his wife was a very attractive young woman. The husband took me aside and said, "I'm sure glad you put that blanket fidelity insurance on my wife. I didn't know there was such a thing. Now when I'm away I don't have to worry about her carrying on with the tenants!"

Just the fact that you require a fidelity bond usually weeds out the dishonest manager. One apartment building I bought had a full house and the resident manager seemed efficient and cooperative, so I was willing to keep her. But she was unbonded. I left a bond application for her to fill out. When I came back the day I took ownership, a tenant greeted me in the manager's apartment. The tenant said the manager had left her in charge and had skipped across the border into Mexico with all the cash collections.

It turned out that the manager had been collecting $270 more each month than she turned in. She charged each of twenty-seven tenants an extra $10 a month for utilities, which the owner paid for. She gave her personal receipt for the $10 utility bill and the owner's receipt for the regular rent. She no doubt would have stayed on until I found her out, except that she was afraid of the bonding company which insured fidelity.

Before you buy a property it pays to check the rent roll with all or at least some tenants to verify that the listed rents are correct. Some unscrupulous sellers list rents higher than those actually collected in order to distort the value upward. In this case, the seller was as surprised as the buyer to learn that all the rents were higher than the rent roll!

MORE INSURANCE

It pays to have burglary and robbery insurance to give both manager and owner peace of mind. Your package fire insurance, of course, should include various extended coverages, such as protection against loss of income, against vandalism and malicious mischief, and against windstorm and water damage to both buildings and furniture. Also, you must have comprehensive liability insurance to protect you against lawsuits that might otherwise devour your assets. Many insurance companies provide substantial discounts by combining all the foregoing insurance coverages, including comprehensive liability, extended fire, fidelity, and burglary and robbery, in one all-inclusive apartment-house policy.

When you go over your insurance program, which you should do at least annually, it pays to take a look at big premium discounts that can be achieved by so-called franchising. This means you can, in certain cases, have a deductible clause for the first $100 to $1,000 or more, whichever amount you select. I save several thousand in annual premiums by having $1,000 deductible on La Peralta. It pays to weigh the certain savings against potential losses. With some coverages the savings are a worthwhile gamble. In other cases the savings are too small to warrant the additional risks.

Some owners spread their insurance piecemeal among a number of friends and business connections. Perhaps they suppose it pays to have as many insurance contacts as possible. But this is a mistake. In order to get the best protection when you need it, at the most reasonable cost, it works out best to turn all insurance over to an expert in the apartment field. Mine was initially recommended through the local Apartment Association. Although he has proved very competent, I annually verify that his deal stays the best by getting competitive bids from at least two brokers who represent other companies.

NEW GIMMICKS

There are always new gimmicks coming on the the insurance market that an alert and conscientious broker, such as mine, can bring to your attention. Sometimes a rival broker will present new ideas which you may consider worthwhile. I give the competitor a chance to bid on my overall package, and I discuss with my present broker the inclusion of acceptable new ideas in my existing policy.

A broker who handles considerable similar insurance can often arrange for bonus riders attached to your policy at no additional cost or for a nominal surcharge. You can include coverage, for example, for little or no cost, by a so-called endorsement, protecting you against suit for illegal entry because you inspect an apartment.

THE MOSTEST FINANCING

A Southern general said, "The way to win battles is to get there fustest with the mostest men and guns."

Certainly the way to win money-making tenants is to get there fustest with the mostest competent staff and profitable improvements. But the way to win financially is to borrow the mostest and pay lastest and leastest.

This means that your goal in financing is to borrow the most that you can safely pay back, and arrange for as long a term and as low an interest rate as can be obtained, resulting in lowest monthly payments. Borrowing the repayable maximum and paying back as little as possible leaves you with the most funds with which to buy more property and make more profitable improvements.

Sometimes you can get good long-term financing at the time of purchase, especially from a seller. Perhaps arrangements can be made for a loan big enough to pay for all projected improvements, usually with an amount to be held back until the improvements are completed. It is more common on older buildings to take over an existing first mortgage which is insufficient to cover total financing requirements. The need for additional loans often results in secondary financing by the seller.

When you want to make improvements, you may be able to pay for them with a new long-term loan based on the projected increased rents, which help to increase the market value. The more common practice is to get shorter term financing to pay for improvements. You might also pay for new furniture or appliances by using a chattel mortgage as security.

Financing easy to obtain is an FHA Improvement Loan to pay for building improvements, equipment, appliances, and furniture. After you make the improvements and raise the rents, then you should shop for a long-term loan to pay off all other loans: the first mortgage; the second mortgage and other subsidiary mortgages, if any; and any remaining loans, such as chattel mortgages. This consolidation into one loan will make your payments considerably lower and conserve in-pocket cash.

Federal savings and loan associations can now lend on the value of furniture in addition to the building and land, making it easier to finance appliance and furniture purchases on a long-term basis. There are many sources for long-term financing. It pays to shop for loans as much as for property, with banks, credit unions, insurance companies, building and savings and loan associations, mortgage brokers, and pension funds.

AVOID INCOME TAXES

Jesus said, "Render unto Caesar the things that are Caesar's." But that doesn't mean you should pay the government a cent more in taxes than you have to!

The property investor pays more than his share of real estate taxes. But he must pass this expense on to tenants. Real estate investment is still encouraged in the United States, and I believe it always will be. With proper accounting, both your pyramiding and operating profits can be comparatively free from income taxes. We should all be thankful that in our American free-enterprise system everyone is encouraged to make a fortune.

Income tax laws keep changing, but I will mention some points significant for property owners, at this writing in 1986, including old and new regulations. It pays to keep interested in changing figures to get the most out of life as an investor, and it is perfectly legitimate to figure taxes to pay the least.

The best chance a property owner has to save operating expenses is to decrease income taxes by taking all the depreciation the law allows. Even though you wind up with a good in-pocket income from your property, this can usually be offset entirely by depreciation. If you use maximum beneficial accounting practices, you should be able to show a depreciation loss sufficient to offset other income.

LEGITIMATE DEDUCTIONS

Interest on your loans is, of course, a deductible operating expense, along with many other items. Some of them are often overlooked, especially by beginning property owners. A number of legitimate expenses are allowable as soon as you become an income-property investor. For example, the law now says you can deduct twenty-one cents a mile for use of your auto for investment purposes by yourself, your family, or your employees. This would cover trips to your property for supervision, and shopping trips to buy supplies and equipment for your apartments or other rental property. Keep track—even if you only send a handyman to the hardware store for a screwdriver!

As an investor you can also deduct for trips to look over prospective properties you are thinking of buying. An income-property owner with many holdings to supervise might deduct the entire expenses of one or more autos. If a car is used for both business and personal pleasure, then it is important to keep detailed records of any business-related use.

As a member of an Apartment Association, you can deduct dues and assessments and the cost of attending meetings, conventions, and seminars sponsored by or related to your association. Your spouse's expenses may be included, especially if you are joint owners. You can also include business-related entertainment expenses. Better keep track of it all! You can deduct the cost of professional magazines and books, such as this one, that add to your investment education and help improve your operations.

If you keep an office in your home you can possibly deduct a proportionate cost of house expenses, including depreciation, utilities, insurance, etc. For example, if you have a five-room house and one room is set aside as your office used exclusively for investment purposes, then you can deduct one-fifth, 20 percent, of your home operating expenses. Expenditures solely for office use can be deducted 100 percent, either as an operating expense or by depreciation. Included are office supplies, such as stationery and stamps, and depreciable equipment, like safes, typewriters, calculators, personal computers, copiers, file cabinets, and desks.

Besides office space, you can deduct for the proportion of your home set aside for storage or repairs for investment purposes. One investor I know has converted his entire double garage into a storeroom and workshop for storage and repair of apartment furniture, supplies, and equipment. All the proportionate cost is deductible.

SHOULD YOU FIGHT RENT CONTROL?

Rental owners should fight the imposition of rent control and continue fighting for its removal. But if it is enacted in your area, it doesn't pay to fight at every encounter with rent control. It pays to take advantage of it to the greatest extent that you legally can. You can make good profits under rent control if you cooperate and work with it as long as it is in effect.

New York investors have told me, "Even though you operated under rent control in the past, you have no idea what it's like now. You Californians aren't living under rent controls today as we have to."

All rental owners thought that rent control was extinct when it was abolished nationally shortly after the end of World War II. Sad to say, it has sneaked back into cities all over the country. It is especially tough and has been challenged as unconstitutional in the California cities of Berkeley and Santa Monica. Rent control is moderately tough in Los Angeles and San Francisco, and also in Oakland, cite of my La Peralta Apartments.

My property managers have agreed with me to follow rent control directions, but to take advantage of every possibility to increase income. Fortunately, continuing improvements allow reasonable increases, and so do vacating tenants. Under livable controls you can rent a vacant apartment at market rates, and it then becomes refrozen at that rate. You are allowed a 10 percent annual cost-of-living increase, and it pays to apply all allowable increases. Under rent controls more increases are made across the board, rather than selectively, usually generating an adequate allowance to pay for increasing costs of operations.

TENANT MAJORITIES RULE CITIES

Rent control has become more widespread because two-thirds of the voters in a typical city are tenants. When rent control goes on the city ballot the tenant majority prevails in establishing shortsighted controls that will reduce rather than increase available housing.

Some owners use rent control as an excuse to make no repairs that can possibly be avoided. Rent control in general drives away investment in new construction that would normally increase rental units. Availability is also reduced by an accelerated conversion to condominium housing and commercial rentals.

OWNER MAJORITIES RULE STATES AND THE NATION

Typical voters statewide and nationally compose a two-thirds majority of economically more responsible owners. They will eventually prevail and override shortsighted city renters. State and national voters, legislatures, and administrators are acting to reduce or eliminate controls. As an example, recent regulations restrict federal financing and guarantees of housing loans to projects free of rent control.

Don't let rent controls discourage you from making good profits! I believe in following a constant program of making improvements and repairs, rent control or not. While rent controls are in affect you can still make money, both in operations and in turnover, if you follow my suggestions to keep making profitable improvements.

ALWAYS COMPETITION FOR FUNDS

Remember, your resident manager is always competing for the dollars of prospective tenants. You're not only competing with other apartment complexes for tenants' rental dollars, but with every merchant and dealer in your area out to make a buck. When a breadwinner gets a promotion, the family may debate the merits of buying a new car, or a boat, or moving into a bigger, more luxurious apartment at an increased rent, or using the increased resources toward purchase of a home.

Even within a household, among husband and wife, there is disagreement about how monies should be spent. Consider the case of one young couple who had just learned of the husband's promotion and raise.

"That's wonderful," the wife exulted in the good news, "and it comes when I really need it. I just came from the doctor's office and he says for my health I should have a fur coat and take a cruise."

The skeptical husband phoned the doctor and asked, "Did you tell my wife to buy a fur coat and go on a cruise?"

"Well, not exactly," the doctor replied. "She had a little cold, and since she stays cooped up in that little apartment and wears those mini-skirts she's so fond of, I told her she should put on more clothes and get some fresh air."

CHAPTER 16

The Wrights Find a Pot of Gold

THE WRIGHTS DISCUSSED how they should capitalize on their rewarding experience fixing up apartment buildings increasing in size to the thirty-unit Silverado. Should they reconsider smaller dwellings like single-family houses, duplexes, and fourplexes? Or should they concentrate on graduating into larger complexes?

Some investors like to specialize in single-family homes and, perhaps, duplexes. Many do quite well continuing with one- and two-unit buildings. In smaller communities such structures may be the only rental investments available.

Specializing in single-family homes and duplexes takes a lot more supervisory time than working with larger buildings, like the eighteen-unit Paradise Apartments and the thirty-unit Silverado, where resident managers handle most operating details.

Property managers find they can make a fair income with 5 percent of the gross receipts on thirty-unit and larger buildings, like La Peralta. For managing an eighteen-unit building like the Paradise they usually charge 6 percent or 7 percent. For managing single-family homes and duplexes they need at least 10 percent of the gross rental income to earn a fair return for their time.

CHALLENGED TO HANDLE LARGER PROPERTIES

The Wrights concluded that it would be more of a challenge to handle bigger properties for which they could afford competent resident managers. They decided to shop for a fixer-upper apartment complex in the range of fifty to a hundred units.

The Wrights double-checked for-sale ads for possibilities, both Norman and Karen reading all ads. Sometimes one would find a potential glimmer in an ad the other had overlooked.

They drove around looking for distress properties and for-sale signs in all the various areas of Metropole, from downtown to the outlying suburbs. They again advised all of their previous real estate sales contacts that they were back in the market, looking for fixer-upper apartments, preferably at least fifty units. Included in their alert search team were Patti Arthur, who had sold them the Spruce Street house, Cindy Seekum, who had sold them the Wildwood fourplex, and Francis Meeker, who had sold them the thirty-unit Silverado.

By the end of 1983, after two months of shopping, the Wrights had found several good possibilities, including three shown them by Francis Meeker. The Wrights made an offer through Meeker for a forty-eight-unit suburban complex, and one other offer for a sixty-unit downtown apartment house. Both offers collapsed because neither a satisfactory price nor satisfactory financing could be arranged.

By the first of February 1984, the Wrights still had not found the right property. Karen said to Norman, "Looks like it's going to take as long to find a really good buy as it does to fix it up!"

On Friday, February 10, the Wrights were both excited by the following for-sale ad in the *Metropole News*.

> *FIND YOUR POT OF GOLD*
> *ON GOLDEN WAY!*
> The Golden Arms Apts.
> Now on the market.

Some lucky buyer
can make a pot of gold.
All you need is a
little fixer-upping.
72 deluxe units.
Good financing.

GOLDEN EAGLE REALTY
Ask for Willis Ames
Phone 367-0488

The Wrights made an appointment to meet Mr. Ames at his office at ten o'clock the following morning. On Saturday morning a beaming, muscular Ames said, "I just put my 'Pot of Gold' ad in the paper and got quite a few calls already. This property isn't going to stay on the market very long. It will save a little time if you just look this statement over before you bring up any questions, then feel free to ask anything you want." He handed each of the Wrights a copy of the following statement.

Golden Arms Apartments,

22100 Golden Way, Metropole, Columbia

Statement of Income and Expense

PRICED TO SELL—$1,600,000.00

Good financing available: minimum down 20% cash, $320,000.00

Owner will finance balance to responsible Buyer at 10% interest, 30-year payout, with wraparound loan. Subject to present 1st Deed of Trust, Metropole Savings & Loan Association. Balance approx. $807,983 (original $900,000) payable by Seller at $6,604 monthly, including 8% interest.

Improvements: 72 deluxe 2-bedroom apartments, contained in 18 4-plexes.

Approx. 1,000 sq. ft. each, totaling approx. 72,000 sq. ft. All partially furnished. All have wall-to-wall carpets, drapes, air conditioning, garbage disposals, 12-ft. refrigerator, built-in stoves. Tenants pay own utilities except for water. 20 × 50-ft. heated pool.

Lot: Choice Golden Eagle rental area, one block south of Golden Eagle Park.

L-shaped lot, approx. 152,100 sq. ft., portion of Golden Acres, Book 36, Map 103. 185-ft. frontage on Golden Way, 660 ft. deep, 285 ft. rear width. (285 × 660 ft. less 100 × 360 ft.)

Gross annual income		$208,488.00
Monthly rent schedule		
February 1, 1984:		
36 2-bedroom apts, upper, at		
$235 each	$8,460.00	
36 2-bedroom apts, lower, at		
$245 each	8,820.00	
Plus coin laundry income,		
owner machines, av.	94.00	
Total monthly income	$17,374.00	

Annual expenses		$52,225.78
Advertising	$ 472.00	
Insurance (Apt. policy, comp., fire & liability)	2,876.00	
Manager & custodian (#1213-C plus $1,000 month)	14,940.00	
Maintenance & repairs	2,132.00	
Taxes	19,846.18	
Supplies & misc.	1,625.28	
Gas (hot water for pool & laundries)	2,368.35	
Electricity (pool filter, laundries, yard & porch lights)	1,672.21	
Water	986.40	
Phone, manager	123.36	
Vacancy allowance	5,184.00	

2½% of rents (usually full)

Total annual expenses $52,225.78

    Net annual income after expenses $156,262.22

    Note: Full-time manager & custodian couple handle pool and yard work and all minor repairs.

    Inspection: Contact Managers Mr. & Mrs. Johnson (Hal & Gloria) Apt. 1213-C Phone 481-4410

    Shown by Golden Eagle Realty
    22310 Golden Way, Metropole, Columbia

    ASK FOR WILLIS AMES
    Phone 367-0488

RUNDOWN APARTMENTS MEAN LOW RENTS AND LOW PRICES

After looking over the statement, Norman Wright asked, "What do you mean by 'a little fixer-upping' in your ad?"

"The owner, Mr. Haddum, has let the place run down. I believe in being frank about it. His wife completely shuns the place. Leaves the management—or I should say mismanagement—entirely up to him. By the same token, that means a good buy for you because the rents are low for this area. No question about it. If you were to go in and clean the Golden Arms up good I bet you could double the income. Just takes somebody with a little foresight and a little gumption. You'll have to see the whole thing for yourself. Let's get in my car and I'll take you right over."

On the way to the Golden Arms Apartments the Wrights asked about financing possibilities. Ames assured them that financing was very flexible for the right buyers, but Mr. Haddum needed a pretty good chunk of cash to pay off his gambling debts.

At the Golden Arms, children of all ages were playing in the parking areas, in the driveways, and on the concrete decks around the pool.

The eighteen buildings were painted white, splotchy all over with barren spots showing the natural gray stucco underneath. The outside walls were accentuated with dark splotches near the ground where the black earth splashed up from sprinkling spotty shrubbery and the bare ground. Complete exterior repainting was badly needed over the apparently skimpy original job.

The tar-and-white-gravel roofs all looked in good condition, with plenty of life remaining in their expected fifteen to twenty years of normal wear. The Wrights asked how old the apartments were, and Ames said about eight years.

A 6-foot-high Cyclone fence surrounded the complex of eighteen buildings. There was no shrubbery against the fence. Some decrepit shrubbery drooped in front and down the sides of each building. There were no lawns except for a scrubby lawn around the pool decks. There were parking spaces between the buildings.

The swimming pool in the rear of the complex was green with algae. Ames said the circulating pump was burned-out. The manager had left it running all night after the pool was pumped dry in order to give the white plaster walls and bottom a good acid cleaning treatment. The pool supply house didn't have the right motor in stock and was waiting for a replacement from the factory. Of course the present owner would pay for it, Ames said.

Ames guided the Wrights to the managers' apartment at the rear of the complex. A buxom silver-haired blonde opened the door. Her heavy makeup partially concealed the fading of her youthful beauty. Ames introduced her as Mrs. Johnson and asked if she or her husband could show some vacant and some rented apartments.

Mrs. Johnson said, "All the apartments are rented. We have master keys, and my husband Hal will be glad to show you as many as you want. He's working on something in the shop we made out of the laundry room for this building."

A stocky and red-faced Hal appeared at Mrs. Johnson's call. The rooms looked spacious in the 1,000-square-foot apart-

ments. The Sheetrock walls in most of them were badly in need
of patching and painting. Refrigerators and stoves in each of the
apartments looked fine, but most of the other furniture in the
"partially furnished apartments" looked quite beaten up after eight
years of wear. Most of the thin carpets were worn through in
hallways and well-used passage areas. Mattresses were lumpy.
Upholstering on sofas and matching chairs was threadbare. Most
of the inspected apartments had one or two children.

MORE NEGLECT MEANS MORE OPPORTUNITY FOR PROFIT

At the rear of each of the eighteen fourplexes an 8-by-12-foot
laundry room projected. Half of these rooms contained an automatic washer and automatic dryer with coin collectors attached.
Several of the washers and dryers had "Out of Order" signs pasted
on top with adhesive tape. Ames said that the laundry machines
belonged to the owner of the apartments and it sometimes took
several days to repair them.

As Mrs. Johnson had said, the laundry room in the managers'
building was used as a workshop. Eight of the laundry rooms
were stacked high with nondescript furniture which Hal Johnson
said had been discarded by tenants. More discarded furniture was
exposed to the elements, piled along with nine unused laundry
tubs between the Cyclone fence and the rear of the buildings.

The Wrights made a thorough inspection of one apartment in
each building. They signaled each other without alerting Ames
as they marched along that there was plenty of profit-making
work to be accomplished. They pointed out obvious problems to
Ames.

When the inspection tour was completed, Norman said, "There's
a lot more work needed than we ever expected. We'll have our
contractor look the place over and see if we can come up with a
reasonable offer."

"A good buy like this isn't going to stay on the market long,"
said Ames driving back to his office. "When we get to my office

why don't we write up an offer, and you can put in it 'subject to satisfactory repair contract,' or something like that. That way you'll have the Golden Arms tied up if Mr. Haddum and his wife accept."

Ames intimated that he expected an offer at or near the full asking price. The Wrights believed that making such an immediate offer would mean a higher price than they could obtain by a slight delay. Their experience indicated probable fixer-upper costs of over $5,000 per building, totaling in the range of at least $100,000. However, they wanted a firm estimate of improvement costs before making an offer.

"We think your property has possibilities," said Karen. "But as my husband said, there's a lot of work that needs doing. And we expect to get credit for it if we buy. You'll just have to be patient and wait until we have a better idea of our repair costs."

ANOTHER RENT-DOUBLING DEAL?

On the way home from the real estate office Norman asked Karen, "What do you think?"

"I hope it isn't bad luck to say so, but I have a strong feeling that Mr. Ames is right and we've got another double-the-rent deal. It's hard to believe that if you keep looking you will find owners who let their properties go to pot. They sure don't have much imagination or they would see that their values slide down if they let their properties go down. They are made to order for fixer-uppers like us."

"I agree. It looks as if we have another tremendous fixer-upper opportunity right up our alley—if we can just buy right and work out good financing."

The Wrights made an appointment with Jack Armstrong to meet them at the Golden Arms Apartments the next Monday morning, February 13. They made a quick inspection of every unit and discussed repair and improvement needs as they went along. They planned to junk the laundry equipment and all the old furniture as tenants vacated, renting completely unfurnished except for stoves and refrigerators. In the meantime, they would arrive at reasonable costs and arrange the financing they wanted to thoroughly renovate all seventy-two apartments inside and out and transform the sickly landscaping.

Armstrong said he could give a firm estimate by the next evening. He arrived with his proposal on Tuesday evening, February 14. It happened to be Valentine's Day, which the Wrights interpreted as a good omen.

A PIECE OF THE ACTION

Jack Armstrong said, "You know I've helped you and quite a few others become rich by handling their improvement work, and I've been wanting to get a piece of the action myself. Like I told you, my wife was too scared to take chances being an owner. We lost all our savings trying to run a little restaurant, and Amy was afraid we'd go broke again buying property. Then one of my carpenters bought a fixer-upper house. He moved in and did what was needed and made a $42,000 profit when he sold. That encouraged one of my handyman helpers to buy a fixer-upper house and he made a $37,000 profit. Amy got jealous about letting our help get ahead of us, so she finally agreed to get on the bandwagon and buy a fixer-upper. We have done real well fixing up a single family home and we just bought a duplex that we can't miss on. Hope you don't mind my competing with you."

"That's great!" said Norman Wright. "We owe you a lot for all the good work you did for us, and we're sure glad to see you get a piece of the action."

"That's wonderful," said Karen. "There's plenty of room for everybody who is willing to tackle fixer-upper property. Hope you're going to continue with reasonable contracting though. Will you?"

"Yes, I figure I can handle both investing and contracting. I'll have to charge a little more because I'll have to put a foreman on each job to take my place. But that won't amount to much, and I'll still be very competitive." Following is the proposal submitted by Armstrong.

Estimate of Proposed Work

Golden Arms Apartments, 22100 Golden Way, Metropole, Columbia

Carpet all halls 72 apts., all 72 living rooms, and all 144 bedrooms	
Install new linoleum all 72 kitchens and dining areas	
Install new indoor-outdoor carpets all 72 bathrooms	$52,000
Complete painting over new and old work, all inside halls and apts., all 18 laundry rooms and all exterior, including 18 2-story buildings and including finished patching of all holes	44,000
Trim shrubbery and kill weeds. Plant Arizona Cypress along all circumference fences. Plant all unplanted and unpaved areas with junipers. Reseed lawn around swimming pool decks	8,500
Overall repairs including electrical and plumbing, sprinklers and lamps	7,000
All first-class labor and material	
subtotal	$111,500
10% contractor overhead	11,150
10% contractor profit	11,150
Total	$133,800
The Wrights added their estimated financing costs of 10 percent	13,380
This made their estimated total including financing costs	$147,180

The Wrights were quite satisfied with Armstrong's previous contracts, but they prudently asked for bids from two other leading contractors. As expected, they considerably exceeded Armstrong's price. One all-union contractor bid $249,000. The other contractor, who was nonunion, bid $159,000.

Norman Wright figured the potential profit if they were able to double the rents, on the basis of all seventy-two apartments being completely renovated and unfurnished.

36 2-bedroom upper apartments × $470 each	$16,920
36 2-bedroom lower apartments × $490 each	17,640
Coin laundry concession 50% of $576 ($8 average × 72)	288
Total monthly income	$ 34,848
Total Annual Income	$418,176

Estimated expenses $52,225.78 plus $245 monthly increase for free managers' apartment, annual increase $2,940

Total annual expenses	$ 55,165.78
Estimated new net annual income	$363,010.22
Present net annual income	156,262.22
Increased annual net income	206,748.00
Increased capital value after improvements	$2,067,480.00

ESTIMATED PROFIT OF 1,400 PERCENT

The estimated capital profit on $147,180 fixer-upper costs would be 1,405 percent or fourteen times the cost of improvements.

Norman showed his figures to Karen, and she said, "Isn't it amazing how the profits mushroom when you deal with larger properties? Of course, we haven't doubled the rents yet, but I think we will."

"In that case," said Norman, "do you realize that the Golden Arms will really produce a pot of gold and make us multimillionaires?"

"It's obvious that the more units we buy the faster we will grow," said Norman.

"You are so right," said Karen. "All we have to do is negotiate to buy right and arrange good financing."

THE FUN OF NEGOTIATING TO SHAVE THE PRICE

"It's like the Silverado—it looks like we would have a good buy even if we have to pay the full asking price," said Norman. "But we can have a little fun negotiating to shave the price. The only apparent problem is to arrange the financing."

The Wrights discussed their various options, basically involving a trade of either or both the Silverado and Paradise Apartments. New financing could be obtained on either or both, arranged to make an advantageous buy of the Golden Arms Apartments. Golden Arms also might be refinanced or taken over with present financing.

Ames insisted that the Haddums must have a minimum of $300,000 cash down. This would pay the realtor's commission of approximately $48,000 at 3 percent of the sale price, and leave the Haddums with $252,000 to pay for some gambling debts and other obligations plus a nominal reserve.

It's fine to buy with nothing down as with the Paradise, if an advantageous, feasible transaction can still be arranged. Better deals can often be negotiated if the buyer meets specific demands for a certain amount of cash. Usually the cash can be raised from refinancing the properties involved, whether they are being bought or sold.

The Haddums' demand for $300,000 cash down could readily be satisfied, the Wrights thought, through refinancing of one, two or three of the properties, the Golden Arms, Silverado, and Paradise, depending on the arrangements made. The refinancing to raise cash could be made a part of the escrow instructions, to be completed as a condition of exchanging properties. This would be a likely arrangement. Or there could be a property exchange concluded with the understanding that necessary financing could be arranged later.

After considering various options, the Wrights chose a simple exchange of equities as their opening ploy. On February 15, 1984, through Golden Eagle Realty, they made an exchange offer of the Silverado Apartments, subject to loans of approximately $375,313, for the Golden Arms Apartments, subject to a loan of approximately $807,983.

The equity of the Silverado, based on the market value of $1,152,348, was approximately $777,035. The Golden Arms equity, based on a market value of $1,562,622, was approximately $754,639. Based on market values, the Wrights' even trade of equities offer represented a bonus to the Haddums of $22,396.

The Wrights' offer represented a value of only $14,982 less than the $792,017 asking price for the Golden Arms equity, based on the listed price of $1,600,000.

WHERE IS THE $300,000 CASH DEMANDED BY THE HADDUMS?

The Wrights reviewed their offer figures in detail with Ames and gave him a complete up-to-date statement on the Silverado. Norman said, "As you know, exchanges are usually valued at market values on all properties. We are offering to exchange equities across the board, so we are giving a bonus of $22,396."

"This looks all well and good as far as your price for the Golden Arms is concerned. But where is the $300,000 cash coming from that the Haddums absolutely demand? It means you either have to sell your Silverado Apartments or refinance either the Silverado or the Golden Arms, or both."

"We could easily arrange for that as part of the escrow instructions," said Karen.

"It would be simpler to go ahead and consummate the exchange," said Norman. "Then each party could arrange for any money he wanted by refinancing. We would be getting a run-down property that needs a lot of fixing up and the Haddums would get a property that is completely in first-class condition. This should appeal to them, since they don't take to fixing up properties. Why don't you submit our offer as we put it to you?"

A LITTLE POINT TO NEGOTIATE

"There's one little point we should take care of before we go any further," noted Ames. "That's the commission. If we trade your property, my boss would want a 5 percent fee based on your listed price."

"You already told us you are charging the Haddums 3 percent, which is plenty for such a big sale," said Norman.

"Yes—you're making plenty there, so you shouldn't charge us anything," said Karen.

"All right, all right. We'll make your fee 3 percent, the same percentage as the Haddums are paying. Let's see—you have listed a market value of $1,152,348. Three percent would be $34,570, wouldn't it?"

"I think you ought to round it to $30,000," said Karen. "That's still a lot of money on top of the Haddums' commission."

"I've earned every cent of it if we make this deal. Tell you what, though. I'll round it to $34,000 and my boss won't okay a penny less. I honestly think we're spinning our wheels offering the Haddums a trade. At least you're offering what looks like a fair price, so I'll give it a try."

THE HADDUMS ARE INTERESTED

The following evening, February 16, Ames phoned the Wrights that he had a progress report and would be right over to discuss it. "I didn't think it was possible that the Haddums would consider your exchange offer," he said. "They were interested enough to

look over the Silverado Apartments and see if there was a possibility of working something out. I showed them the Silverado,
and you can bet I kept putting in my little sales pitches. After
all, the place is in real nice shape!

"After their inspection the Haddums said that basically they
didn't mind taking over the Silverado in its tip-top condition.
Among other considerations they just don't like fixer-upper work
themselves. And there was a tax advantage to trading for the
Silverado. There's only one problem, which they have repeated
over and over. They've got to get $300,000 cash. Now they say
it must be arranged as part of the conditions before closing the
escrow. They emphasized that they need almost $50,000 for our
broker's fee and $250,000 clear besides."

"You can easily borrow $300,000 on the Silverado," said Nor-
man.

STIPULATING THE FINANCING

"The Haddums wanted me to arrange for necessary financing in
advance and then write a new sales contract," said Ames. "I'm
sure there's plenty of equity in the Silverado to borrow the $300,000
cash for the Haddums, one way or another. Maybe a new first,
a new second, or a wraparound loan. But I could go to all the
trouble of securing financing and then the whole deal could collapse. It would be better to button up the deal as soon as possible
'subject to arranging the necessary financing.'"

"That's a good idea," said Norman. "Go ahead and write up
a modified exchange offer on that basis."

"What about our financing to pay for all our Golden Arms
improvement work?" asked Karen.

"Yes—as long as the agreement stipulates financing, we should
have it both ways," said Norman. "The exchange should be subject to the Haddums getting their cash financing and subject to
the Wrights getting the financing we need to pay your broker's
fee and improvement costs."

"That sounds fair enough," said Ames. "How much do you need?"

"About $200,000," said Norman.

"I don't see any problem there. We'll just add to your exchange offer 'subject to the Haddums receiving a minimum of $300,000 cash from refinancing the Silverado Apartments, and subject to the Wrights receiving a minimum of $200,000 cash from refinancing the Golden Arms.'"

Norman said, "Of course, you should add 'subject to all loan arrangements being satisfactory to each borrower.' The exchange basically swaps equities with all funds from refinancing to go to each buyer."

"Of course. I'll just make the changes in your offer. You folks can both initial the changes, and I'll take the agreement over to the Haddums for their signature tomorrow."

NEGOTIATING THE CONTINGENCY OF TIME

The next evening, February 17, Ames phoned the Wrights. He said everything was okay with the Haddums except for one little contingency, and he would be right over to discuss it.

"The Haddums said they couldn't let this drag on forever," he said. "They want a sixty-day limit for getting the financing. Otherwise the deal can be canceled. You don't need to worry about that. I believe sixty days will give us plenty of time."

"I don't think we should agree to sixty days," said Karen. "We might have everything almost ready to go by then and have it canceled."

"We might make it in sixty days," said Norman. "But I believe we should stipulate 120 days. That would give us a more comfortable leeway."

"You could agree to the sixty days," said Ames. "Then the agreement can always be extended if that isn't enough time. If you agree to the sixty days you will have the place tied up, and nobody else can come in and snap up the place ahead of you."

"I don't like the idea of being pushed into too short a time allowance," said Karen. "We might feel forced to accept some financing we don't really like."

"Sixty days is too short," said Norman. "We want you to tell the Haddums we should have 120 days to allow plenty of time. Then we can all try to get the financing settled as soon as possible."

Ames tried to get the Wrights to agree to a maximum time limit of ninety days, but the Wrights insisted on trying for 120 days.

The next afternoon Ames phoned the Wrights. "The Haddums said they would extend the time to ninety days, and that's their absolute limit. If I were you I wouldn't haggle about any more time, but go ahead and snap up the ninety-day provision before the Haddums change their minds. After all, I won't get paid a cent unless we close the deal. You can bet I'll really work hard to get the financing settled. We should have it all arranged in sixty days, and ninety would give us plenty of leeway."

Ames was quite happy when the Wrights agreed to ninety days. He brought the papers that evening for the Wrights to initial the final counteroffer already initialed by the Haddums. This completed the exchange agreement on February 18, 1984, giving all parties ninety days to complete financing which would turn the Silverado over to the Haddums and the Golden Arms over to the Wrights.

As it turned out, all necessary financing was arranged for fifty-eight days after signing of the exchange agreement. The exchange of the Silverado for the Golden Arms was consummated in escrow on April 16, 1984.

MINING $300,000 CASH FROM THE SILVERADO WITH A WRAPAROUND

The Silverado first mortgage held by the Biggerts was paid down to $257,294 effective April 16. The second-mortgage rehabilitation loan held by the Capitol National Bank was paid down to $117,383. Realtor Ames reviewed with the Haddums the chief Silverado options available.

A new third mortgage of $300,000 would be quite costly, involving interest up to 20 percent and a bonus in the 20 percent range of $60,000, which would mean paying for a $360,000 loan in order to obtain $300,000.

A new first mortgage of approximately $700,000 would be comparatively easy to arrange. It would produce the $300,000 in cash, pay off both existing loans (totaling approximately $374,677), and pay loan costs. Interest at that time would be about 14 percent, making payments including interest on a thirty-year loan of $8,294.

The bank would probably take a dim view of leaving the first mortgage intact and increasing its $117,383 rehabilitation loan to a second mortgage of approximately $450,000. The bank would want 14 percent interest on such a subsidiary loan.

The most feasible arrangement to retain the favorable first mortgage and keep the bank in a secondary position would involve a new wraparound loan of $700,000. This would override but be subject to the continuing first mortgage of approximately $257,294. The bank would actually advance the difference of $442,706 less $117,383 for paying off the rehab loan, delivering $325,323 less loan costs in cash to the Haddums.

Since the bank would be paying off its 12 percent interest rehab loan and would get the benefit of the 9 percent first mortgage, it would probably agree to a new thirty-year wraparound with a 12 percent interest rate, making monthly payments of $7,200 including interest.

A WRAPAROUND LOAN USUALLY BENEFITS ALL PARTIES CONCERNED

The mechanics of a wraparound loan would require the Haddums to pay the bank $7,200 a month. The bank would credit the entire payment to the wraparound loan. Then the bank would pay from it to the Biggerts their $2,092 monthly payment, leaving the bank with a net of $5,108. The Biggerts would not be affected, except that they would be somewhat more certain of receiving their payments when due.

The lender bank could grant a lower interest rate because it would receive 12 percent on the entire $700,000 wraparound loan and pay only 9 percent on the $257,294 first mortgage.

The borrower Haddums receive the benefit of a 12 percent interest rate on the entire loan of $700,000, instead of paying 14 percent on a conventional second mortgage or all-new first mortgage.

NEGOTIATING THE LOAN FEE

Ames presented the wraparound proposal to Real Estate Vice President Yeager at the Capitol National Bank. Yeager said that they had an up-to-date appraisal on the property and there would be no problem in granting the application for a $700,000 wrap-around loan, which would be subject to the approximately $257,294 first mortgage.

Yeager said, "I trust the borrowers know that a loan fee is required. We would normally charge 5 percent on this type of loan. Since you are paying off our rehabilitation loan I can make it 3 percent of the new $700,000 loan."

"That looks reasonable," said Ames. "I'm sure the Haddums would be willing to pay something like that. It should apply only to the funds advanced, of course. You've already received a healthy fee for the rehab loan, which is now being paid off. The Haddums would expect to pay a fee only on your new funds. Can't you adjust your fee so I can get their approval and button this up?"

After a little sparring Yeager agreed to apply the 3 percent loan fee only to funds advanced of $325,323, after paying off the bank's $117,383 rehab loan. This reduced the new loan fee to $9,760. After paying for incidentals the Haddums received a bonus of about $15,000 more than their $300,000 requirement.

THE GOLDEN ARMS GENERATES CASH FOR ITS OWN IMPROVEMENT

Ames told the Wrights that he had arranged many attractive financial deals through Abe Ketchum, president of Metropole Savings and Loan, which held the present first mortgage on the Golden Arms. Other lenders could be contacted if necessary, but probably the best arrangements could be made through the present lender, which would be most anxious to finance improvement work as it would enhance its security in the Golden Arms.

"In fact," said Ames, "with your equity over $750,000, I'm sure I could get you $400,000 or so in new loan funds if you want it."

Norman said, "After we improve the Golden Arms we might try for maximum refinancing so we can use the money to buy and fix up more property. We could get a lot more, of course, after we fix up the Golden Arms. Right now we would save interest and fees by getting only what we need to pay for improvements and your commission."

"It doesn't hurt to add a little reserve," said Karen. "We might plan on getting $210,000 instead of $200,000."

Ames said, "I'll try to talk Mr. Ketchum into the best possible deal to raise your $210,000."

Ames planned to discuss various potential options and costs with Ketchum.

Ketchum said, "I'll be glad to advance the $210,000 you want. There are several ways we could do it, of course. The best solution would be to arrange a new first loan of approximately $1,020,000. The interest for the new loan would have to go from 8 percent to 12 percent."

"That's way out of line! You're trying to get rid of your 8 percent loan and sock it to the Wrights instead of being reasonable. I'll have to arrange the $210,000 financing elsewhere and keep your loan at 8 percent unless you can do a hell of a lot better."

Ames and Ketchum carried on a lively discussion concerning various subsidiary financing possibilities, including a second mortgage and a wraparound loan, and comparable costs. They failed to complete an agreement except that they would both reconsider the various options and meet again the next day.

Ketchum finally accepted the dual arrangement that Ames found most favorable for the Wrights: to increase the present first mortgage to its original amount of $900,000, producing about $93,000 after escrow costs; and to obtain the balance by a $120,000 second-mortgage rehabilitation loan, less a $3,000 loan fee.

With this arrangement Ketchum suggested that the interest on the first loan should go from 8 percent to 10 percent, and he would charge a loan fee of only 1 percent.

Ames protested, "That's too high a penalty when you're only putting up about $90,000 cash. You ought to be satisfied with 8½ percent interest and no loan fee on this portion when this loan was already $900,000 originally."

Ketchum agreed to 9 percent interest on the entire first loan of $900,000, and to waiving any loan fee on this advance. It was agreed that the payments would increase to $7,242 monthly including interest, paying off the loan in thirty years.

The most favorable arrangement that Ames could obtain on the subsidiary $120,000 rehabilitation loan required a 2½ percent loan fee and 14 percent interest, payable in twenty years at $1,492 monthly including interest. Payments would start on June 1, 1984. Interest would apply when the money was advanced to make progress payments on the improvement work.

Ames made several trips between the buyers and the lenders to complete favorable negotiations to refinance both the Golden Arms and the Silverado. As noted, the exchange escrow was completed on April 16, 1984, the date that the Haddums took possession of the Silverado and the Wrights took possession of the Golden Arms Apartments, on their way to becoming multi-millionaires.

FIXING UP THE GOLDEN ARMS TURNS INTO A GOLD MINE

The Wrights netted $93,000 from refinancing the first mortgage. They received $117,000 from the $120,000 subsidiary improvement loan after deducting the 2½-percent loan fee of $3,000. This total loan fee was a welcome saving compared to the original forecast of $13,380.

From the dual loan proceeds of $210,000 the Wrights allocated $133,800 to pay Jack Armstrong's contract and $34,000 for the realtor's commission. This left them with $43,200 to deposit in a new Metropole Savings money market account, available for further investment or improvements.

It took six and a half months, till November 1, 1984, to complete all the contracted improvements, as some of the work was delayed by tenants who refused admittance until they moved. It took five months longer to complete other projected changes and apply the planned new rent schedule, with a slight upward revision.

At the beginning of the improvement program, rent raises of $100 monthly were given to all tenants. Most tenants stayed. The thirteen who refused admittance were given eviction notices. All of them and eleven other tenants moved over a three-month period. Any vacated apartments were completely fixed up at once and rented at the new schedule.

As tenants moved, the manager encouraged them to take the house-owned furniture with them except for the stove and refrigerator, provided they took all furniture, including both desirable and damaged items. Then the apartments were rented unfurnished at the new schedule as planned, except for leveling the upper and lower rents.

The previous owners had rented the upper apartments on the second floor for $235 and the first-floor apartments for $245, figuring the convenience of the ground floor most desirable. The Wrights found the choice about equal when they had both a lower and upper vacant at the same time. Some tenants preferred the ground floor for convenience, but as many preferred the added security of living on the second floor. So the Wrights rented all the vacated and refurbished apartments at the same schedule of $490.

All old tenants remaining when the improvement work was completed were raised to $470. Most of them moved within an additional three months. All tenants paying less than $490 on February 1, 1985, were raised to that amount.

BONUS STOREROOM INCOME

The Wrights arranged with their coin laundry operator at the Paradise and Silverado to provide new washers and dryers in nine of the laundry rooms and pay the Wrights 50 percent of the gross income. The operator said the old beat-up machines previously owned by the Haddums were of no value to him, but he would cart them away as a courtesy.

The Wrights figured they might as well receive some return for giving the machines away; about half of them were operating and half needed repair. Karen phoned three charitable organizations, Goodwill Industries, the Salvation Army, and the Society of St. Vincent de Paul. She offered the free operating machines in exchange for having all remaining discarded furniture and laundry machines hauled away. Two of the charities refused to take anything but the usable laundry machines and furniture. The spokesman for the third said his organization would repair some of the discarded furniture and equipment and would gladly haul it all away in exchange for the usable items.

The Wrights decided to reserve one of the nine remaining laundry rooms for a workshop and one for house storage. The other seven would be rented to the tenants for their personal storage.

THE GOLDEN ARMS LEAPFROGS IN VALUE

By April 1, 1985, the following monthly income schedule was in operation at the Golden Arms Apartments:

72 2-bedroom apartments × $490	$35,280
50% of gross coin laundry receipts of $612	306
7 tenant storerooms × $40	280
Total monthly income	$35,866
Gross annual income	$430,392

The previous amount for annual expenses, $52,225.78, increased only $245 monthly for the free manager's apartment, an annual increase of $2,940, to $55,126

This raised the new net annual income to	$375,226
The new capital value after fix-up leapfrogged to	$3,752,260
Total loans outstanding effective April 1, 1985	1,009,564

(First mortgage $900,000 April 16, 1984, payable $7,242 monthly including 9% interest. Principal balance $895,056. Second mortgage improvement loan $120,000 advanced from April 16, 1984, to November 1, 1984. Payable $1,492 monthly including 14% interest. Principal balance $114,508.)

The Wrights' net equity in the Golden Arms Apartments $2,742,696

THE WRIGHTS ARE WORTH $3,266,338

The Wrights figure their complete investment statement as follows.

Estimated equity in 72-unit Golden Arms Apartments $2,742,696
>   (Market value $3,752,260 less outstanding loans $1,009,564)

Estimated equity in 18-unit Paradise Apartments   416,536
>   (Market value $675,000 less outstanding loans $258,464. Since the November 1, 1983, statement in Chapter 14, 17 additional monthly payments on the two mortgages have reduced the principal on both loans. The first mortgage is reduced to $143,740 and the second-mortgage improvement loan to $114,724, totaling $258,464.)

Money market balance, Capitol National Bank   48,187
>   (November 1, 1983, balance of $41,569 plus 10% interest of 6,618 for 17 months)

Money market balance, Metropole Savings & Loan Association   47,736
>   (April 16, 1984, deposit of $43,200 from Golden Arms refinancing plus 10% interest of $4,536 for 12 months)

Credit union balance $11,183
>   (November 1, 1983, balance of $7,017 plus $200 additional monthly savings for 17 months of $3,400 and 6% interest of $766)

> Total net worth $3,266,338

The Wrights bought their first investment property, the Spruce Street house, on March 10, 1981. Forty-nine months later they have accumulated net investment assets of $3,266,338. In just over four years they have become multimillionaires and approached the six-year goal in Chapter 3 of $3,545,197.

As long as they continue applying their eagerness to gain an eight-figure net estate before resting on their laurels, it looks like they should have no difficulty in accomplishing the seven-year goal in Chapter 3 of over $10 million.

JOYS OF RETIREMENT

My wife loves to shop, and this is fine with me. When I retired from the telephone company many years ago, she was determined to replace my boring old business suits with more colorful leisure clothes.

"I'm looking for something youthful," Lucille told the salesgirl in the men's department of her favorite store. "Something wild in a pair of slacks."

"Oh," sighed the salesgirl. "Aren't we all?"

CHAPTER 17

Opportunity Is
Always Knocking

SOME PEOPLE WORRY about a depression and others worry about inflation. The President and the Congress are worried about both, so we had better consider them. We are bound to have periodic ups and down in the economy. Have you noticed that the stock market goes up and slides down, but real estate values generally keep going up?

MAJOR DEPRESSION OR INFLATION?

In the big downturn a few years ago the stock market skidded 40 percent, with a loss of $70 billion. At the same time, real estate values continued to increase at about 8 percent a year to a total of over $3 trillion.

As mentioned earlier, some gloom-mongers tell you the economic world is coming to an end, sliding to hell on a catastrophic depression, coming any day now. They have been predicting imminent economic collapse for years. Nothing like the severity of their predictions has happened or will happen.

Nothing that you can conceive is absolutely impossible, but

it is almost impossible to have another major depression as in 1929. There are many built-in safety factors that we did not have in 1929. At that time there were no economic cushions like Social Security, Unemployment Compensation, Farm Price Supports, and Federal Deposit Insurance to alleviate income losses.

In 1929 you could buy stock with only 10 percent down, and a slight dip in the market wiped you out. Most stock today is bought with considerable cash, with a minimum of 50 percent down. Even when the stock market recently lost $70 billion, the heavy cash margins prevented individual bankruptcies.

WHEN FIVE YEARS WAS A LONG-TERM LOAN!

The big difference in property safety is that most mortgages then were for only three years, a practice many have forgotten. Five years was considered a long-term loan! Only the interest was usually paid, and the whole original loan fell due at once. If money was tight you could not renew your loan, and this forced foreclosure under the laws then in effect.

I ought to know, because that's what happened to my dad, when I was eight. He lost his Wilderville, Oregon, farm when he couldn't renew a three-year improvement loan, then moved to California to work as a farm laborer. He worked in orange-packing sheds in Porterville and in Anaheim near the site of the present Disneyland. Then he got a job taking care of an orange grove in Yorba Linda. There our neighbors included a family with a name slightly similar to ours, the Nixons.

Now foreclosure laws are more lenient and you are given more time to make good. Real estate loans are usually self-amortizing, paid off in monthly installments from the income. Some real estate loans have balloon payments, but with most of them you just keep paying monthly until the loan is paid in full, and you have no problem of renewal. Usual payoff terms run from twenty to thirty years. Quite a contrast with the three-year term faced by my Dad!

PUT SOMETHING INTO PROPERTY

Another question I'm often asked is, "Does real estate success depend on inflation?"

No, absolutely not! Property values will always increase with general inflation. Inflation looks like a continuous spiral ahead that will keep pushing up real estate values about 5 percent a year for the foreseeable future. But mine is not a program based on inflation. I constantly advocate putting something into the property, building or remodeling to achieve competitive rentals on it, or fixing it up to increase its value. Or you might increase income and resulting value merely by changing or improving the management!

"As you sow, so shall you reap," the Bible truly says. If you put judicious improvements into property, like the Wrights, then you can earn virtually certain profits.

WIN/WIN PLEASES ALL PARTICIPANTS

It makes me angry when sour-grapers who don't know any better say, "You can't make money without cheating somebody." That's the beauty of real estate transactions if they are handled properly. All real estate deals should mean WIN/WIN—the buyer and the seller should both be happy that their desires have been well satisfied. With all the favorable buys made by the Wrights, each seller was satisfied.

Making money doesn't mean that you have to deprive somebody else, for most of the wealth that you create through real estate investment and improvements would not be there at all except for your efforts.

"PLEASE DON'T PUBLISH BOOK!"

My books and lectures have brought Lucille and me many heartwarming experiences. We both love to learn how well so many thousands are doing by following our example and guidance. Many students all over the country like the Wrights have told us how we have inspired them to change their lives and become financially independent.

Meeting new friends everywhere we go certainly changes our lives and makes us very grateful. We want to keep encouraging others as much as we can. When questions of any nature are asked, we seldom believe in holding back, but try to give as complete and helpful an answer as possible.

When I told friends that I was writing a book about my real estate experiences and conclusions, several said, "Please don't publish any books until we get ours!"

Like my old friends, some of my new readers worry that the market will run out of opportunities and there won't be any more fixer-uppers available. A common complaint: "Surely your first readers have picked out all the good buys."

I say, "Not to worry." Many of my students are snapping up good buys, and they certainly have a big advantage. After reading my books they know more about buying and taking care of property than the average real estate broker.

Prices are continuing to go up, but this is only relative. The real estate investment field is continually expanding, and there is plenty of room for all who apply themselves. There are four major factors working away for you who yearn to invest in real estate. Besides time and inflation, previously mentioned, they are technology and the stork!

TIME, INFLATION, TECHNOLOGY, AND THE STORK

Relentless *time* keeps wearing away every day as shelters decay. Remember, there are fifty million dwelling units in need of some renovation, and twenty million that need major rehabilitation. And remember that *time* drops half a million units a year below the slum line, so they need to be demolished or completely rebuilt.

Inflation will continue to expand values at an average of about 5 percent a year.

Technology increases production per man-hour, which results in ever higher incomes. Median family earnings have doubled in the last ten years to over $25,000, so tenants can pay for the improved housing they have always wanted.

The busy *stork* has slackened a bit, but still creates a need for well over a million additional dwelling units every year.

When you improve housing, the benefits spread to many fields, covering materials and labor. You can make a substantial profit as a fixer-upper investor. You also provide better living for tenants, and a sounder economy for the whole country.

THERE WILL ALWAYS BE OPPORTUNITY

In just about every lecture audience for several years now, some students, like Norman and Karen Wright, tell us they have already made their million. Others are close to it, and many have made a fine start toward being wealthy. Yet every day, as mentioned earlier, some pessimists keep saying there is no opportunity anymore. Back during the Depression, many experts, such as our economics professor mentioned earlier, said, "The days of opportunity are over."

One of the biggest thrills for Lucille and me after my first book came out was an invitation from Fresno State College, where we met. I was asked to lecture to the student body on my just-published best-seller, *How I Turned $1,000 into $1 Million in Real Estate—in My Spare Time.*

Sharing the platform with Lucille and me were the mayor of Fresno, the president of Fresno State College, the dean of the college, and lo and behold in a seat of honor our old economics professor!

The mayor said the city was proud and the president said the college was proud of Lucille and me for becoming their nationally known representatives.

Guess what our economics professor said?

"I'm proud to say that I taught Bill Nickerson everything he knows about economics! I'll have to admit that Bill and Lucille were smart to save and invest during the Great Depression. I should have started investing back there when they did. But now that we have better times, it's *too late* for opportunity!"

Just think, *you* can find it, but that poor professor, like a lot of other prophets of doom, will *never* find opportunity! All he can say is "I should have."

Opportunity in real estate investment is always there, waiting for you. Let it change your life so you can become wealthy. Then you can look back later and say, "I'm glad I did it!" instead of "I should have."

OPPORTUNITY IS IN YOUR STATE OF MIND

All you have to do is recognize opportunity and take advantage of it. I can tell you of thousands of opportunities that have been won, and some that have been lost. I can assure you that thousands of fixer-upper opportunities in real estate offer you fabulous profits at virtually no risk.

Often opportunity is there and we don't see it. Or we may see it and pass opportunity by. Some skeptics, like our economics professor, never recognize an opportunity until after they have missed it!

I have come to the conclusion that to a great extent, opportunity is in your state of mind. Opportunity does depend on your personal attitude—whether you really want to recognize it and make progress. As previously mentioned, opportunity is always there for you, yesterday, today, and every day, in good times or bad. Opportunity in this free-enterprise land of America knocks not just for the favored few, but for all who aspire to better themselves. And opportunity knocks not just once, but many times. All you have to do is open the door that is offered to you.

WHEN OPPORTUNITY KNOCKS

Three priests went on a fishing trip at a church retreat on the coast. There was a small island offshore. One of the priests, called Pious, said he wanted to row out to the island where he could be alone and commune with God. The others said the water looked rough and he'd better not go. Pious said, "Don't worry. God will take care of me."

The other two started surf-fishing on the main beach and noticed the wind and waves were increasing. They heard over their portable radio that a hurricane was headed their way. They rowed across the rough water to the island where Pious was on his knees praying.

"You'd better leave the island right way," they said. "A big hurricane is coming."

Pious said, "Please go back and don't bother me anymore. I'm talking with God right now, and he will take care of me."

The two priests had a hard time rowing back to the mainland, praying all the way. A big storm blew up and covered the island with water. Pious drowned and went straight to Heaven. He demanded to see God face to face.

"You failed me," he accused God. "I told everybody you would take care of me, and here you let me drown."

"My son," said God, *"You failed to recognize opportunity.* Don't you know that *I* sent those two men to save you?"

Index

About the Author

William Nickerson, a Californian, began his career in real estate at the age of twenty-eight. He had managed to save $1,000 of his earnings as a telephone company employee and made a down payment on a house. Two years later he and his wife traded that home for a pair of apartments. After working twelve more years for the telephone company and operating rental property as a sideline, he managed to pyramid his net estate to a million dollars, and after that to three million, and finally into five million dollars! He retired at the age of forty-two to concentrate on managing his property, with time out for gardening, swimming, hunting, fishing, traveling, writing and lecturing. Bill Nickerson and his wife, Lucille, whom he married when they were students at Fresno State College, live on Monterey Bay in California. They have two children, Robert and Nancy, and five grandchildren.